Genghis Khan

Biography of Genghis Khan
Founder of the Mongol Empire

(How Genghis Khan's Brutality Created One of History's Largest Empires)

James Butler

Published By **Regina Loviusher**

James Butler

All Rights Reserved

Genghis Khan: Biography of Genghis Khan Founder of the Mongol Empire (How Genghis Khan's Brutality Created One of History's Largest Empires)

ISBN 978-1-7387533-1-4

No part of this guidebook shall be reproduced in any form without permission in writing from the publisher except in the case of brief quotations embodied in critical articles or reviews.

Legal & Disclaimer

The information contained in this book is not designed to replace or take the place of any form of medicine or professional medical advice. The information in this book has been provided for educational & entertainment purposes only.

The information contained in this book has been compiled from sources deemed reliable, and it is accurate to the best of the Author's knowledge; however, the Author cannot guarantee its accuracy and validity and cannot be held liable for any errors or omissions. Changes are periodically made to this book. You must consult your doctor or get professional medical advice before using any of the suggested remedies, techniques, or information in this book.

Upon using the information contained in this book, you agree to hold harmless the Author from and against any damages, costs, and expenses, including any legal fees potentially resulting from the application of any of the information provided by this guide. This disclaimer applies to any damages or injury caused by the use and application, whether directly or indirectly, of any advice or information presented, whether for breach of contract, tort, negligence, personal injury, criminal intent, or under any other cause of action.

You agree to accept all risks of using the information presented inside this book. You need to consult a professional medical practitioner in order to ensure you are both able and healthy enough to participate in this program.

Table Of Contents

Chapter 1: Why Genghis Khan's Leadership Matters Today 1

Chapter 2: The Rise Of Genghis Khan 5

Chapter 3: Building A Winning Team 12

Chapter 4: From Warrior To Statesman . 16

Chapter 5: The Art Of War 23

Chapter 6: The Power Of Communication 26

Chapter 7: Leading Via Way Of Example 49

Chapter 8: Legacy And Influence 57

Chapter 9: Applying Genghis Khan's Leadership Strategies To Modern Business And Life 67

Chapter 10: Early Life 77

Chapter 11: Military Tactics And Conquests 87

Chapter 12: Impact On Mongol Culture . 96

Chapter 13: The Silk Road 105

Chapter 14: Legacy In Modern Times... 121

Chapter 15: The Early Life Of Genghis Khan From Humble Beginnings To Rising Power 141

Chapter 16: The Formation Of The Mongol Empire Strategies And Tactics.............. 145

Chapter 17: Genghis Khan's Military Campaigns Conquests And Triumphs... 149

Chapter 18: Genghis Khan As A Visionary Leader Political And Social Reforms 154

Chapter 19: The Legacy Of Genghis Khan: Impact On History And Culture 157

Chapter 20: The Myths And Legends Surrounding Genghis Khan: Separating Fact From Fiction 162

Chapter 21: Genghis Khan's Personal Life: Family, Relationships, And Legacy........ 166

Chapter 22: The End Of An Era: The Death Of Genghis Khan And The Aftermath ... 170

Chapter 23: Genghis Khan's Influence Today Lessons And Insights For Modern Leaders 174

Chapter 24: The Controversies Surrounding Genghis Khan Criticisms And Defenses 179

Chapter 1: Why Genghis Khan's Leadership Matters Today

Genghis Khan become a twelfth-century Mongolian warrior and commander who constructed the Mongol Empire, which at its peak turn out to be the most important non-prevent empire in records. His manage has had a great effect on the globe and remains applicable nowadays. Here are some reasons why Genghis Khan's control topics these days:

Military Tactics and Strategy: Genghis Khan modified into famed for his particular navy strategies and approach, which allowed him to triumph over large regions and bring together a exceptional empire. His processes protected using pace, mobility, and wonder to outmaneuver his foes, and he modified into moreover identified for his use of mental conflict and espionage. Today, many army commanders don't forget

Genghis Khan's strategies and thoughts as a blueprint for fulfillment on the battlefield.

Political Organization: Genghis Khan turned into a grasp of political employer, and he built a gadget of governance that became quite green and successful. He developed a centralized management that have grow to be based totally totally on benefit, rather than own family or extended circle of relatives relationships, which served to hold balance and order in the course of the empire. This fashion of control continues to be relevant in recent times, and plenty of current worldwide places have patterned their political structures at the ideals that Genghis Khan pioneered.

Cultural Exchange: Genghis Khan became identified for his tolerance of numerous cultures and faiths, and he fostered cultural alternate all through his realm. He perception that variety modified into a power, and he advised his people to observe from and understand numerous cultures. This statistics of cultural interchange remains critical in recent times, as globalization and the net have made it much less complex than ever to engage with humans from numerous cultures and origins.

Economic increase: Genghis Khan's control also had a primary effect at the monetary growth of the globe. His kingdom superior a massive community of industrial channels, referred to as the Silk Road, which related China with Europe and the Middle East. This network served to foster economic growth and improvement, and it moreover helped to transmit thoughts and inventions within the direction of severa cultures and areas.

Leadership Philosophy: Genghis Khan's leadership philosophy emphasizes the importance of institution spirit, loyalty, and discipline. He felt that a splendid leader must inspire devotion and determination in his subordinates, and he valued vicinity and difficult artwork specially else. This precept continues to be relevant in recent times, and masses of cutting-edge-day leaders examine Genghis Khan's management style as a model for achievement.

In conclusion, Genghis Khan's control subjects these days due to his imaginative combat strategies, his effective governmental corporation, his encouragement of cultural interchange, his have an effect on on financial growth, and his control philosophy. His legacy maintains to inspire leaders at a few stage within the globe to in the intervening time, and his effect on data can't be puffed up.

Chapter 2: The Rise Of Genghis Khan

The emergence of Genghis Khan is a fascinating narrative of imaginative and prescient, patience, and management. Genghis Khan, whose true name modified into Temujin, end up born in 1162 in Mongolia. He changed into the son of a frontrunner of a tiny Mongol extended circle of relatives, and his boyhood became defined with the aid of way of the usage of poverty and strife. However, he grew to grow to be one of the best conquerors in facts and based totally the most vital non-forestall empire in history, accomplishing from the Pacific Ocean to the Danube River.

Genghis Khan, the writer, and primary emperor of the Mongol Empire got here to electricity within the twelfth century thru a aggregate of navy electricity, strategic alliances, and outstanding perseverance.

Genghis Khan's youth turn out to be marred with the resource of war and tragedy. He become born right into a tribe of nomadic herders, and his father modified into poisoned while he become high-quality 9 years antique. He and his own family were driven out via the usage of using their tribe and left to fend for themselves within the harsh steppes of Mongolia. These early critiques without a doubt taught Genghis Khan the importance of perseverance and self-reliance.

Despite those hurdles, Genghis Khan unexpectedly set up himself as a exquisite warrior and commander. He solid ties with neighboring tribes and in the long run advanced a devoted following of warriors. He furthermore displayed excellent tenacity inside the face of setbacks and disappointments. For instance, in a unmarried early combat, Genghis Khan emerge as kidnapped and enslaved thru a rival tribe. However, he managed to break out and shortly reassembled his squaddies, in the end beating his captors in a decisive fight.

Genghis Khan's endurance changed into furthermore visible in his navy techniques. He grasped the want of converting to changing situations and have become prepared to observe from his shortcomings. He have become a grasp of guerilla methods and diagnosed the need of mobility and quickness in conflict. He additionally grasped the significance of records and intelligence series, and he made use of a massive network of scouts and spies to maintain beforehand of his fighters.

In summary, Genghis Khan's perseverance come to be a big detail of his climb to energy. It enabled him to stand as much as the limits and disappointments that got here his manner, modify to converting conditions, and sooner or later acquire a exceptional and strong empire that lasted for centuries.

Genghis Khan's number one ambition changed into to unify the Mongol tribes and construct a effective Mongol Empire. He sought to accumulate a centralized administration that is probably based totally totally on meritocracy instead of tribal connections. He additionally predicted a powerful strain that might be able to conquering adjoining kingdoms and developing the empire's frontiers.

Genghis Khan believed in a hierarchical society in which the governing elite may additionally have normal authority over the inferior commands. He idea that it come to be the placement of the ruling elegance to attend to and protect the humans below their authority. He moreover believed in religious tolerance and gave freedom of worship to all faiths finally of the empire.

Overall, Genghis Khan aimed to collect a excellent and wealthy empire that might stay on for hundreds of years and characteristic a protracted-lasting mark on the globe.

One of the critical instructions we are able to draw from Genghis Khan's ascent to energy is the need of having a easy imaginative and prescient. From an early age, Genghis Khan had a imaginative and prescient of a unified Mongol america, which may be powerful enough to combat the invading armies of China and unique surrounding international places. He diagnosed that this best may additionally need to only be carried out via solidarity and electricity, and he went approximately forming alliances with other tribes and clans in the vicinity.

Genghis Khan changed into moreover a draw near of resilience. He persevered severa setbacks and obstacles within the route of his lifestyles, which includes the killing of his father, the abduction of his spouse, and the betrayal of his closest supporters. However, he in no manner gave up or overpassed his purpose. Instead, he exploited those setbacks as possibilities to take a look at and expand, modifying his mind and techniques to triumph over the hurdles in his way.

Another lesson we may additionally draw from Genghis Khan's ascent to energy is the significance of notable management. Genghis Khan turned into a charismatic and inspirational leader who modified into able to inspire and inspire his human beings to carry out superb matters. He led through instance, displaying his valor and bravado at the battlefield and treating his humans with apprehend and justice.

Genghis Khan turn out to be moreover a first-rate strategist and tactician. He emerge as able to alter his strategies to the terrain and instances he encountered, the usage of marvel attacks, feints, and distinct strategies to defeat large and higher-organized forces. He moreover found out the need of logistics and supply traces, and he spent considerably developing a community of deliver depots and delivery networks to serve his navy.

In quit, the ascent of Genghis Khan offers us with terrific classes in vision, resilience, and control. Genghis Khan's capacity to unify the Mongol tribes, his fortitude within the face of problem, and his control and strategic competencies all done a essential detail in his fulfillment. These teachings are however relevant nowadays and can be applied to a large style of sports, from commercial enterprise and politics to private development and increase

Chapter 3: Building A Winning Team

Genghis Khan changed into famed for his awesome navy victories and the constructing of an terrific Mongol Empire. One of the vital motives that precipitated his success have become his recruiting approach and popularity on range, which helped him increase a winning organization.

Genghis Khan knew that to make bigger a extraordinary navy, he needed to trap guys who had plenty of talents and strengths. He did now not restriction his recruiting to contributors of his tribe or extended circle of relatives however alternatively sought out human beings from wonderful tribes and clans who had crucial abilities and abilties.

In addition to recruiting people from numerous tribes and clans, Genghis Khan also commonplace human beings from various cultural and spiritual backgrounds. He said the significance of range and felt that humans from various backgrounds can also additionally bring glowing perspectives and thoughts to the table.

By enlisting guys with various backgrounds, Genghis Khan have become able to set up a powerful and adaptable military that become able to adapt to severa conditions and terrain. The Mongol military became normal of riders, archers, and infantry, every with its particular strengths and capabilities. Genghis Khan moreover pressured the significance of education and region, which served to assure that each person have become capable of execute their manner properly.

Another number one difficulty that contributed to Genghis Khan's success changed into his ability to set up a enjoy of togetherness and devotion among his military. He dealt with his men with admire and justice, and he rewarded them for his or her devotion and valor at the battlefield. He moreover highlighted the rate of collaboration and entreated his men to artwork together to gain their goals.

Genghis Khan's recruiting approach and attention on range not only helped him develop a remarkable navy pressure however moreover enabled him to set up connections with one-of-a-kind tribes and clans in the area. By forging partnerships with diverse tribes, Genghis Khan modified into capable of growth his authority and feature an impact on and in addition assemble his kingdom.

In prevent, Genghis Khan's recruiting method and recognition on variety achieved a essential issue in his achievement. By enlisting guys with numerous backgrounds and talents, Genghis Khan come to be able to set up a powerful and adaptable army which have become capable of adapt to numerous situations and terrain. He moreover advanced a feel of brotherly love and commitment amongst his squaddies, which helped to assure their victory on the battlefield. These commands in recruiting and variety are however relevant in recent times and can be implemented to a vast shape of occasions, from commercial organisation and politics to sports activities and training.

Chapter 4: From Warrior To Statesman

Genghis Khan modified into now not handiest a awesome warrior, however he additionally advanced right into a geared up flesh presser who have come to be able to administer and manage his massive kingdom correctly. His transition from a warrior to a statesman includes numerous essential reasons and events.

Firstly, after years of war and conquest, Genghis Khan observed the want for a more strong and lasting device of rule. He knew that his empire required a centralized manage to guarantee peace and order, supply important necessities to the populace, and foster monetary increase. Therefore, he built a office work with appointed officers tasked with overseeing the empire's affairs.

Secondly, Genghis Khan knew that the conquest and dominion of neighboring areas could not be perpetuated through military pressure by myself. To guarantee the devotion of his people, he needed to adopt policies that might advantage them. He, consequently, supported change and company, constructed roads and bridges to useful resource trade, and provided protection for traders, which contributed to financial prosperity in the empire. Additionally, he abolished feudalism and changed it with a benefit-based totally completely tool of appointment, wherein appointments had been primarily based totally on an person's ability and now not their social role or history. This enabled the empire to emerge as greater inclusive and allowed for upward social mobility.

Thirdly, Genghis Khan located out the necessity of global circle of relatives members in retaining peace and safety internal his dominion. He created diplomatic contacts with neighboring global locations, which helped him maintain peace and safety on his borders. Through global members of the family, he modified into capable of negotiate alliances and treaties, which further enlarged his empire.

Finally, Genghis Khan became a visionary chief who grasped the need of prolonged-time period making plans. He emerge as able to assume future dangers and issues and made movement to lower them. For instance, he spent notably on infrastructure, like irrigation systems, which enabled agricultural growth, diminishing the empire's dependency on nomadic herding. This reduced the threat of famines, that might have eroded his empire's stability.

In surrender, Genghis Khan's alternate from a warrior to a statesman come to be a final consequences of his interest of the need for a sturdy and sustainable device of management, his interest on monetary growth, his beauty of global own family members, and his visionary management. These attributes permit him rule and administer his big empire successfully, assuring balance, wealth, and increase.

financial ruin 5:Conquering New Territory: Lessons in Strategic Planning and Execution

Genghis Khan changed into one of the maximum a achievement army commanders in records, noted for his capacity to triumph over and amplify his empire at an top notch rate. His fulfillment may be because of his strategic making plans and execution, which enabled him to efficaciously use his property and overcome many hurdles. Here are a few awesome methods in which strategic making plans and execution performed a vital component in Genghis Khan's conquest of recent territories:

Building a effective army: Genghis Khan found out the need of getting a robust and disciplined military that would bear any problems. He spent drastically in education his troops and in the advent of advanced military techniques. He additionally ensured that his army become properly-prepared with the most state-of-the-art weaponry and technology, giving them an advantage over their opponents.

Developing alliances: Genghis Khan observed out the want of alliances and partnerships in conducting his desires. He strove to form alliances with robust neighboring tribes and empires, the use of international relations and clever marriages to create connections of allegiance. This allowed him to defend his barriers and increase his electricity past his number one areas.

Exploiting flaws in his adversaries: Genghis Khan have emerge as a wonderful strategist who modified into able to use the weaknesses of his foes to get the higher hand in combat. He meticulously tested the terrain, the processes utilized by his foes, and their vulnerabilities, and then designed a plan of assault that could take benefit of these variables. This enabled him to overcome a long manner larger armies and seize new areas.

Utilizing era: Genghis Khan have become an early adapter of new era, the usage of superior siege engines, consisting of catapults and trebuchets, to interrupt the partitions of opposing castles. He furthermore employed horses to first-rate gain, using them to transport great distances rapid and to release wonder assaults on unsuspecting foes.

Establishing powerful governance: Genghis Khan knew that the key to preserving manipulate over his giant nation come to be to growth an effective tool of presidency. He shaped a centralized government that emerge as accountable for amassing taxes, maintaining law and order, and executing his recommendations. He also decided on unswerving and expert humans for essential posts, imparting him the functionality to rule efficaciously even in rural places.

In summation, Genghis Khan's success may be traced to his capability to correctly prepare and execute his military expeditions. He long-installed a effective military, made alliances, exploited flaws in his competition, employed technology, and installed a a success government. This enabled him to overcome new areas at an splendid price and assemble really one in all the biggest empires in information.

Chapter 5: The Art Of War

Genghis Khan have become a amazing thinker and tactician, and he invented a selection of recent army strategies and techniques that allowed him to conquer and dominate large territories. Here are some of the important military plans and techniques that he deployed in his campaigns:

Psychological Warfare: Genghis Khan became a grasp of intellectual struggle, and he applied worry and intimidation to subjugate his fighters. His recognition for violence changed into well-known, and he regularly carried out surprise attacks and killings to encourage terror in his foes and energy them to submit.

Mobility and Speed: One of Genghis Khan's number one navy property became his capability to installation his navy fast and cowl great distances. He deployed his cavalry to notable advantage, frequently launching marvel assaults and flanking strategies to seize his foes off-shield.

Diversionary Tactics: Genghis Khan became proficient at the usage of diversionary strategies to mislead his adversaries and create confusion. He could from time to time release a feint assault to lure the enemy's interest some distance from his major army, permitting him to release a marvel assault from a few other path.

Siege Warfare: When fighting strongly defended cities or castles, Genghis Khan have to frequently set up siege battle strategies. He need to surround the metropolis or fort, reduce off deliver routes, and mount a non-stop assault to wear down the defenders.

Decisive fights: Genghis Khan regularly tried to engage his opponents in decisive fights, wherein the surrender end result could decide the save you of the warfare. He have to meticulously select the terrain and location his forces to maximise his advantages, and then unleash a concerted onslaught to weigh down the opposition.

facts collecting: Genghis Khan discovered out the fee of gathering expertise approximately his competitors, and he have to often installation spies and scouts to obtain statistics about their strengths, weaknesses, and methods. This helped him to put together his expeditions and fights extra effectively.

Flexible Command Structure: Genghis Khan had a bendy command shape that enabled him to conform to converting situations and react rapid to unexpected occurrences. He may want to regularly supply obligation to his subordinates, allowing them to take self sustaining motion as required.

Overall, Genghis Khan become a incredible strategist and tactician who employed a combination of army strategies and techniques to carry out his goals. His capacity to conform to converting conditions and his willingness to take measured dangers were essential factors in his military achievement.

Chapter 6: The Power Of Communication

It changed into no twist of fate that Marco Polo's famend day enjoy to China befell in a few unspecified time in the future of the Mongol Empire's apex inside the 13th century. His crew of Venetian traders crossed an overland course between the Middle East and China on what should extended later be termed the Silk Road. Their tour through the treacherous terrain could slightly have been feasible without the tool of manage, identified to historians as Pax Mongolica, that the empire had enforced over valuable Asia.

Polo's corporation journeyed underneath the auspices of the Mongol monarch and Yuan dynasty emperor Khubilai Khan, the grandson of the Mongol Empire's founder ruler or "khan," Genghis. The sponsorship took the shape of an unusual passport. According to Polo's story, they have been given a "Tablet of Gold on which turn out to be inscribed that [they] ought to be supplied with everything needful in all the countries via which they need to bypass — with horses, with escorts, and, in short, some thing they must require." With this tablet, Polo's birthday party turn out to be capable of depend on the large infrastructure that the empire maintained within the route of crucial Asian change routes.

The Venetian investors have been some distance from by myself of their use of this infrastructure. By the time they reached Cambaluc, the wintry weather capital of the Yuan dynasty at the region of modern-day Beijing, they observed out that numerous European customers have been before them.

The large suburbs of Cambaluc, steady with Polo, "hotel the remote places traders and tourists, of whom there are generally notable numbers who've come to deliver gives to the Emperor, or to sell articles at Court, or because of the truth the metropolis offers so nicely a mart to attract shoppers." Separate resorts have been created for buyers from diverse regions of the globe, consisting of "one for the Lombards, a few one of a kind for the Germans, and a third for the Frenchmen."

These direct links among Europe and China appear to have been completely new phenomena, something that had no longer came about earlier than Pax Mongolica. "Before this era, we do now not have proof of direct change amongst Europe and China," says anthropologist Jack Weatherford, writer of Genghis Khan and the Making of the Modern World.

It is hard to magnify the ancient significance of Pax Mongolica. Its foundation had come at a first-rate charge. In conquests that pushed the Mongolian Empire to China in the East and to the Danube River within the West, the Mongol army may additionally have massacred upward of forty million human beings. Yet Pax Mongolica presented a reasonably strong weather for the increase of worldwide trade and the go-fertilization of cultures and knowledge that got here with it.

Spices, tea, porcelain, and silk traveled west, on the facet of several Chinese technical breakthroughs. Gold, medicinal writings, and astronomical tomes moved east. These new interactions had large repercussions and were taken into consideration by way of manner of way of 1 historian due to the fact the "onset of world statistics."

Genghis Khan, Administrator

Genghis Khan, born under the call Timüjin, modified into an unusual preference to reconcile the warring Mongol tribes of his the united states of the us, a remarkable deal much less build a large empire. The destiny emperor end up the son of an outcast circle of relatives – a circle of relatives deserted with the useful resource of its members of the circle of relatives to perish on the steppes. Yet it appears that naturally he grew to count on that he changed into divinely destined to unite the planet — all of the u . S . A . Beneath Tengri, the sky deity of his shamanistic spiritual manner of lifestyles. In a upward thrust terrific with the aid of terrific political and army capability, he endured to conquer a prolonged succession of frequently more powerful warring parties.

What might be as extremely good is that this guy with little formal schooling and sincerely limited interest of the outdoor global could probably show to be an effective administrator. Breaking with Mongol way of lifestyles, Genghis have turn out to be a fervent recommend of meritocracy.

To fight intra-Mongol tribal disputes, he prepared his navy and most of the surviving people into gadgets of 1,000. He tended to sell and demote merely on simple performance, with very little interest to tribal affiliations.

A large trouble Genghis confronted modified into the growing numerical disparity between the conquerors and the captives. "He had an army of one hundred,000 and he dominated over hundreds of hundreds of thousands of humans," adds Weatherford. "There isn't any way you could reign over such pretty a few humans basically thru using pressure with this sort of notably tiny navy.

It's honestly no longer manageable." To supplement his navy prowess, he trusted non-Mongol advisors to supply the data and people to run his developing realm. As a technique of preventing indigenous assets of authority in conquered areas, Genghis and his successors often called in propose from other lands. Such end up the situation in China, wherein Khubilai depended substantially on Muslim advise from treasured Asia out of contempt for the close by Chinese Mandarin elite.

One of the vital tendencies of Genghis and his instant successors have become their receptivity to new thoughts. Without their structures to rely on, the Mongol leaders examined a fervour to apply fresh information and practices.

They mixed numerous structures, regularly choosing pragmatic answers. In the initial tiers of the empire, the Mongols' earnings from obtained areas came from the prizes of victory (struggle loot, army requisitioning, and tribute). By Khubilai's time, but, they'd constructed a far greater prepared tax tool.

The series and management of conflict spoils and taxes throughout such big regions necessitated big file maintaining, as a end result their clerks employed the abacus for computations and relied on inventions from Arabic and Indian mathematics (such as the variety 0 and terrible numbers). Effective governance moreover desired the ability to reliably degree time across a long way-flung provinces that finished severa calendars, so

Khubilai based totally the Academy for Calendrical Studies and a printing bureau that mass-synthetic calendars.

The Mongol us of a have come to be entire of juxtaposition. In their military conquests, the Mongols met opposition with savage violence. Yet after gaining energy, their control over conquered territory might be extra complex. In the "Yasa" prison device that Genghis set up to complement traditional Mongol law, the loss of life sentence changed into widespread. Acts of thievery and treachery had been punished with harshness — however the Yuan prison code that the Mongols constructed in China contained about half of the form of capital offenses because the Song dynasty law that it succeeded, and the lack of lifestyles sentence appears to were imposed substantially seldom on civilians.

The Mongol invasion and career have been catastrophic for Chinese agriculture. Large segments of the rural populace have been slain or enslaved, and maximum of the surviving farmers have been trouble to arbitrary taxes and the turning in their lands into grazing and looking regions. Yet unique of Khubilai's measures, inclusive of the deliver of social coverage in the direction of crop failures and natural calamities, replicate a sincere state of affairs for the welfare of his countrymen. According to Marco Polo's testimony, "If the humans are bothered with the useful resource of manner of any dearth thru destructive seasons, or storms or locusts, or different like calamity ... No taxes are exacted for that three hundred and sixty five days; nay extra, he reasons them to be provided with corn of his very very own for meals and seed."

Trade Promoter

The Mongols depended drastically on trade, even in advance than the appearance of their empire. As a nomadic human beings whose livelihood relied on herding and looking, that that they had now not anything in the way of agency. Although they made some smooth devices, it seems that they had few weapons producers, potters, or weavers. They traded often with their friends in China and crucial Asia, generally presenting animals and animal-based totally definitely objects in move back for craft gadgets and food.

With the upward thrust in their empire, the Mongols' enthusiasm for exchange changed into heightened through the way they employed to break up the spoils of conquest. Their common tool of stocks, termed "khubi," have become institutionalized with the resource of Genghis Khan. Under the affiliation, every member of the royal own family become entitled to a part of riches from every section of the empire. The shares had been paid in kind: Mongols who reigned in Persia would in all likelihood deliver spices, metallic, diamonds, and pearls to their equivalents in China, at the same time as the rulers in China may supply porcelain and medicine to Persia.

The conveyance of conflict plunder emerge as now not confined to gadgets, for the reason that Mongols realized the importance of having human beings with expertise and capabilities at their disposal. Even on events while the Mongols ought to kill maximum of the population of a captured usa, the Mongol troops may also select out up artisans, interpreters, physicians, astronomers, and mathematicians to be dispersed throughout the empire.

The khubi machine fostered exchange for the cause that beneficiaries of in-type bills might definitely are looking for to update as a minimum part of their allocations for opportunity gadgets. Combined, the allocation gadget and its ripple outcomes on trade provided a regular go along with the glide of commodities and people among the Middle East and China.

Even inside the direction of instances of violent strife among various sections of the empire (and there had been many), the go with the flow of products grow to be commonly now not impeded for extended. The commonplace interest inside the dispersal of battle plunder and the interchange of merchandise thru alternate appears to have trumped conflicting pursuits.

The Mongols also aimed to stimulate exchange via growing the social position of buyers, granting them strategic inducements and equipping them with a enormous infrastructure and a awesome quantity of protection. The Mongols' thoughts-set toward investors stood in sharp assessment to that of the Chinese, whose social structure earlier than the Mongol-dominated Yuan dynasty located investors best one level above bandits. The Mongols officially boosted the popularity of investors in China to the very best diploma of all occupations, sincerely in the returned of government officers.

"The Chinese step by step acquiesced to Mongol practices," says Morris Rossabi of the City University of New York, who has written appreciably on Mongol records. "That is, they embraced the notion of traders, and the placement of traders stepped forward throughout that era and China in no way went returned. During the Ming dynasty, as quickly as the Mongols departed, buyers grew increasingly effective and respected."

Genghis Khan ought to regularly supply tremendously splendid conditions in his direct touch with buyers — and his son and straight away successor, Ogodei, became even more kind. "When a carrier employer got here to him, Ogodei ought to pay them double, triple what they asked for," recounts Weatherford. "He did that due to the fact he have end up searching for to inspire trade." An greater enticement for buyers changed into the issuance of special passports that provided the holders with safety, housing, delivery, and immunity from nearby taxes and price lists. Marco Polo's golden tablet become the splendid stage of them.

Network Builder

The Mongols advanced a large tool of roads, canals, and postal stations. They inside the starting did so for army motives, however the ensuing network finally facilitated alternate. The postal gadget, called the Yam gadget, modified right into a form of medieval pony particular with stations placed at periods of 20-30 miles. At each station, an "arrow messenger" should mount a glowing horse and experience to the following station at a complete gallop.

According to Marco Polo's account, "At every of those stations used by the messengers, there may be a large and good-looking building ... With amazing beds and all different vital articles ... On some of those posts taken collectively there are greater than 300,000 horses saved up ... And the amazing houses ... Are more than 10,000 in range."

The Yam postal system have become devised specially for the benefit of the Mongols' communications tool, however they also extended it to buyers. For passport-protective merchants, which encompass Marco Polo, the Yam device supplied crucial manual.

Yet the Yam device's rate to investors hinged at the protection that the Mongols want to offer alongside the routes. "The massive obstacle to open exchange emerge as safety because of the reality the trade routes crossed a whole lot of risky territories," says economist Kevin O'Rourke of New York University Abu Dhabi, co-writer of Power and Plenty: Trade, War, and the World Economy inside the Second Millennium. "One of the principle reasons the Mongols had been so useful to exchange have turn out to be that their unification of large chunks of Eurasia supplied human beings with safety." Indeed, the Mongol military-operated and maintained troops along the complete Yam system.

Financial Innovator

The Mongols relied substantially on foreign places traders as entrepreneurs to behavior their corporation. The exchange and cash-lending partnerships they fashioned were called the Ortoq machine, a term that derived from the Turkic phrase for "accomplice." Ortoq partnerships have been comparable in lots of respects to trendy limited partnerships due to the fact a primary's criminal responsibility became capped at the amount of the real investment.

Ortoq partnerships arose pretty early at some stage in the reign of Genghis, and by the point of Khubilai's reign, maximum Mongol-ruled territories that bordered the sea had started to lease partnerships for maritime exchange. This coincided with Khubilai's big increase of China's maritime fleet. "The Ortoqs helped reduce dangers in case a few thing went wrong," says Rossabi. "If one merchant financed an entire task, and the caravan or deliver failed to make it, he'd be wiped out. But if you unfold the danger, no character would undergo dramatically."

Women finished a dominant feature within the Mongol aspect of the Ortoq partnerships. "Mongol men have been now not supposed to be worried with the accumulation of wealth. They have been not supposed to be concerned with some thing past war, religion, and looking animals," says Weatherford. "Women dealt with cash and wealth and the buildup of merchandise. And consequently, the ladies have been worried with the trading device of investors."

The Ortoq system helped Mongol ladies convert the spoils of war into cash, which they used to shop for luxurious consumption devices or lend at interest. Lending cash need to have been specifically appealing, for the motive that, unencumbered thru the usury criminal hints of the Islamic and Christian worlds, the Ortoqs reportedly lent coins at a compound annual rate of a hundred percent.

Khubilai substantially expanded using paper cash in China. The foreign places cash issued under his reign — the Zhongtong Chao — have become ostensibly backed via silver, and it stored its rate in the early years after its advent. Marco Polo found that the foreign exchange changed into regular within the direction of the empire, mentioning, "Nobody, but vital he might imagine himself, dare to refuse [it] on pain of lack of existence." But the evidence indicates that more measures were required to keep its fee.

In the early years, the authorities periodically supported the overseas cash via purchasing for it lower lower returned with silver. The government appreciably applied what amounted to exchange controls. According to Marco Polo's account, "All consumers coming back from India or awesome countries, and bringing with them gold or silver or gems or pearls, are prohibited from selling to truely every body however the Emperor." Occupants of the empire had been in addition prohibited from searching out and promoting silver amongst themselves. The foreign exchange's rate fluctuated over the years with the forces of supply and call for, in the end depreciating considerably at a few degree in the later years of the Yuan dynasty because the regime's monetary situation deteriorated.

The Legacy of Pax Mongolica

There is a robust agreement amongst specialists that Pax Mongolica impacted international information. The time of relative balance, extended spherical 1250-1350, bearing in mind an splendid drift of products and thoughts. In Power and Plenty: Trade, War, and the World Economy in the Second Millennium, O'Rourke and his co-writer Ronald Findlay of Columbia University cross to date as to assert that "globalization ... Began with the unification of the primary Eurasian landmass thru the Mongol conquests."

Many Chinese improvements had positioned their way from China to the Middle East and Europe in advance than Pax Mongolica, silk and porcelain amongst them. The Byzantines had gotten silkworm eggs and began their silk enterprise as early due to the truth the sixth century, at the equal time as archeologists have lately uncovered Chinese porcelain at the Iberian

Peninsula dating to among the ninth and eleventh centuries.

But there may be little trace of direct conversation amongst Europe and China earlier than the thirteenth century. In The Mongols and Global History, Rossabi believes that "The thirteenth century witnessed the number one direct and private contact among Europe and China."

Pax Mongolica affected the globe in numerous tactics. It delivered new devices to Europe, inclusive of textiles like satin, damask silk, and muslin. It moreover allowed for the interchange of technology. With Mongol help, Muslim physicians acquired know-how of Chinese pharmacology, even as Chinese clinical doctors found surgical capabilities from their colleagues within the Middle East. On the much less exquisite side of the ledger, the Mongol switch of gunpowder, a Chinese innovation, to the Western global expedited the history of European conflict. Increased lengthy-distance exchange moreover aided the unfold of risky ailments, which include the bubonic plague.

Yet arguably the most vital effect of Pax Mongolica emerge as from the huge profits that it showered on a achievement customers. Trade, whether or not or not or not over land or water, turned into a excessive-chance, excessive-praise commercial organization. Power and Plenty is a tale of the manner a single a achievement cargo repaid a service issuer for the lack of severa distinct ships.

The potential for oversized earnings gives a giant incentive to limit shopping for and promoting costs and risks through the development of new exchange routes. By whetting the European hunger for change, Pax Mongolica supported the adventures of Vasco de Gama and Christopher Columbus, which acted as springboards to the contemporary worldwide – with all its breakthroughs and carnage.

But the influences of Pax Mongolica were hardly ever symmetric. Europe - a commodities exporter in the back of China and the Middle East technologically — profited pretty from the alternate of thoughts with China. And while the Mongols slaughtered many knights in Hungary, Europe's function usually shielded it from the brunt of the Mongol invasion. Conversely, China's advantages from the go together with the glide of thoughts were very minor, and it carried a significantly better weight from the Mongol invasion and profession.

Chapter 7: Leading Via Way Of Example

Genghis Khan modified into a ancient parent famed for his control and army capability, however he furthermore displayed private responsibility and integrity in numerous techniques. Here are some subjects we are capable of take from him:

Take obligation to your moves: Genghis Khan held himself accountable for his picks, every suitable and horrific. He did now not make excuses or blame others for his shortcomings.

Keep your word: Genghis Khan become famed for fun his commitments and following agreements. He valued loyalty and anticipated the same from all and sundry around him.

Lead via example: Genghis Khan led from the the the front and was prepared to do what he required of his guys. He did no longer expect people to perform anything he emerge as now not prepared to adopt himself.

Be honest: Genghis Khan emerge as famed for his honesty and integrity. He became open together with his fanatics and did now not mislead them or control them for personal benefit.

Have a strong moral code: Genghis Khan had a difficult and fast of values and mind that he lived through. He believed in justice, equity, and treating others with apprehend.

Hold people responsible: Genghis Khan held his commanders and officers responsible for their acts. He could not tolerate corruption or ineptitude and would update people who did no longer fulfill his requirements.

Overall, Genghis Khan's teachings on personal responsibility and integrity may be summed up in the principle of leading with dignity and respect. By accepting duty for our moves, keeping our phrase, essential with the useful aid of instance, being sincere, having a robust moral code, and maintaining people responsible, we may additionally emerge as higher leaders and individuals.

It is honestly smart to lease care whilst looking for to comply with schooling from information to offer agency. Having furnished this warning, we will though challenge to do exactly that: As a questioning workout, what might also additionally need to Genghis Khan be capable of teach us in recent times? He became, in the long run, an early globalist, founding an empire, the Mongol Empire, which in the long run spanned from China to Central Europe.

Initially a petty king with few adherents, Genghis Khan have grow to be stronger below the protection of To'oril. As a topic (expect company) to a more powerful king (purchaser), Genghis Khan in the long run were given stronger (like early Microsoft promoting software program program thru

IBM PCs). Once To'oril believed that Genghis Khan had gotten too powerful he attempted to oppose him, however with the beneficial resource of then it changed into too past due.

Be a well-known manager: To'oril, Jamaqa, and the opportunity Mongolian competition of Genghis Qan lacked his skills as a manager and did now not have his appeal. People came to Genghis Khan to serve him out of preference.

Genghis Khan knew his catch 22 situation nicely. He knowledgeable a Taoist monk: '...I honestly have fulfilled the task of conquering ... the globe and my dominion are acquainted. I actually have little abilities ultimately I am keen on clever parents, considering them like my brothers.' He granted positions of authority to humans of many ethnicities, now not sincerely Mongols.

Integrity: Genghis Khan required a hundred% integrity or maybe predicted a person serving an enemy lord to do so to the extraordinary of his skills. He refused to admit humans into his service who had betrayed their earlier grasp, arguing that one that had as quickly as been faithless could not be relied on. A city that had surrendered and in a while grew to become towards him want to anticipate no compassion.

Task orientation: He knowledgeable his youngsters: 'The importance of an hobby is composed in doing it to the stop.' His whole profession became an extended string of specific sports efficaciously completed. He had no early vision of ordinary conquest.

If he had a methodical method, it changed into to deal with the minor desires earlier than moving at once to the principle ones. The Mongol 'increase' into the Near East end up initiated thru the disrespectful conduct of Mohammad II of Khwarizm in the direction of Genghis Khan. Unable to tolerate this, Genghis Khan took a hundred.000 troops on a 4,000-kilometer westward ride to punish Mohammad.

Obsession with employer and tool: Genghis Khan spent big time putting in location shape and strategies and usually changing and refining them.

Genghis Khan had many distinct key traits and conduct, but the 5 described proper here possibly carry a experience of the individual and his sports sports.

Genghis Khan died in 1227. His dominance have become such that the succession proceeded without hassle as Genghis Khan favored it. He had in his service a tremendous commander named Sube'etei. He remained lively for two a long term after Genghis Khan went away. Sube'etei had an inherent ability to hire innovative techniques to build up tons much less costly triumphs.

He turned into also restless, inclined to attack a ways off goals. In time he conquered vital China similarly to East Europe. Penetrating throughout Central Europe, his columns neared Vienna and Venice earlier than returning domestic. Here is a closing lesson of Genghis Khan; have a stressed and clever strategist in your provider.

Can Genghis Khan inspire the enterprise chief of these days? You determine.

If you are familiar with the concept of the truthful method then you definitely truely definately can be capable of recognize the leadership attributes of the Great Khaan. Fair approach is stated as an powerful manage method within the cutting-edge control philosophy. The importance of the truthful manner is established to its give up end result this is (1) agree with a few of the group individuals and (2) willingness to collaborate for the team voluntarily. The honest approach consists of three critical thoughts which can be:

(1) participation of group contributors in the alternatives that impacts them that is termed the engagement precept.

(2) every team member is informed why very last picks are made as they may be that is called the principle of explanation. And

(three) clarity of expectancies

It is famous reality that the Great Khan had a council composed of nine of his closest friends from boyhood time/ generals which embody Subutai Jebe, Mukhulai (or Mugali), and so forth.

So all critical picks had been taken sincerely in a communication with these 9 generals. Every standard had particular understanding of why this sort of choice is taken. And ultimately, all battle trophies were shared flippantly a number of the 9 generals so each famous knew what he might assume.

This machine come to be great at that time as no different leader was employing this concept. Compared to how other kingdoms were managed the Great Khan come to be a super deal greater progressive and revolutionary appreciably in terms of distributing riches among the generals. There are plenty greater times that could mean successfully that the Great Khan modified into an exceptional leader.

Chapter 8: Legacy And Influence

Genghis Khan come to be the founder and number one emperor of the Mongol Empire, which at its pinnacle, spanned from China to Eastern Europe. He is noted for his military triumphs, inventive strategies, and control abilities. Some of the legacies of Genghis Khan encompass:

Military Conquests: Genghis Khan is famed for his military conquests, which helped grow the Mongol Empire to its excellent quantity. He adopted novel navy strategies which encompass the use of a cavalry, which enabled his military to transport rapid and cowl vast distances. He moreover entreated his warriors to consist of new generation, along aspect siege conflict and gunpowder.

Cultural Exchange: Genghis Khan encouraged cultural trade and tolerance during his dominion. He blanketed freedom of religion, fostered the arts, and encouraged the flow of ideas throughout severa civilizations. The Silk Road trade routes, which linked Asia with Europe, have been made greater stable and extra reachable beneath his reign, bearing in mind greater trade and cultural interchange.

Administrative adjustments: Genghis Khan undertook administrative changes that helped to control the massive areas of the Mongol Empire. He built a benefit-based totally system for appointing officers, set up a prison code, and brought a uniform system of weights and measures. These changes helped to collect a more efficient and structured empire.

Legacy in Modern Times: Genghis Khan is regarded as a photo of Mongolian delight and identity. His reminiscence remains recognized in Mongolia, wherein he's venerated as a countrywide hero. In addition, his military techniques and leadership skills have been studied and replicated through army commanders at some stage in facts.

Overall, Genghis Khan's impact is complicated, embracing each military conquest and cultural interchange. His effect on worldwide facts is terrific, and his legacy is still felt in gift times.

Long term questioning

Long-time period wondering had a wonderful detail in Genghis Khan's success as a pacesetter. He have become a visionary chief who had a strong facts of his desires and worked strategically to acquire them.

Some techniques wherein lengthy-time period wondering helped Genghis Khan emerge as a notable leader are:

Strategic planning: Genghis Khan had a clean vision of his long-term targets, which included unifying the Mongol tribes and building a effective empire. He mounted a strategic plan to reap the ones dreams, which comprised setting up a effective army, adopting new army generation, and conquering surrounding areas.

Flexibility: Despite having a robust long-time period purpose, Genghis Khan modified into moreover adaptable in his approach. He have turn out to be prepared to regulate his strategies counting on converting situations, including the terrain, weather situations, and the strengths and weaknesses of his combatants.

Persistence: Genghis Khan have become a affected character and chronic leader who determined out that mission his prolonged-term desires may also want to require time and art work. He turn out to be now not discouraged via screw ups or hurdles and persevered to strive in the route of his targets even in the face of trouble.

Succession making plans: Genghis Khan additionally had an extended-time period technique for succession, making sure that his empire may also want to hold to prosper even after his loss of existence. He picked certified leaders to supervise numerous sections of the empire and created a smooth line of succession for his successors.

In summation, Genghis Khan's achievement as a frontrunner modified into due in element to his capability to suppose and put together correctly for the long time. He had a smooth imaginative and prescient of his goals and worked continuously to obtain them, at the same time as despite the truth that being bendy and adaptive in his approach. His long-time period thinking moreover includes getting prepared for succession, assuring the continued flourishing of his empire even after his loss of life.

How modern-day-day businesses can also additionally consist of Genghis Khan's prolonged-term thinking technique

Modern corporation executives may moreover moreover take numerous useful instructions from Genghis Khan's long-term thinking method, collectively with:

Developing a smooth vision: Genghis Khan had a strong vision of his long-term objectives and worked relentlessly to gather them. Modern enterprise executives need to similarly have a clean imaginative and prescient of their enterprise corporation's goals and goals, and paintings strategically to gain them.

Strategic planning: Genghis Khan installation a strategic plan to benefit his targets, which included organising a effective navy, adopting new era, and conquering surrounding regions. Similarly, current company leaders need to have a strategic plan that defines the measures required to accumulate their desires.

Flexibility: Despite having a easy long-term intention, Genghis Khan become flexible in his approach and prepared to modify his strategies relying on converting conditions. Modern business enterprise leaders must similarly be adaptive and bendy, eager to pivot and modify their method as required.

Persistence: Genghis Khan changed into a affected person and persistent chief who discovered out that project his long-time period targets ought to require time and art work. Modern organization leaders need to similarly be tenacious and not give up effortlessly, mainly inside the face of losses or stressful situations.

Succession making plans: Genghis Khan had a long-time period method for succession, making sure that his empire might also preserve to prosper even after his loss of lifestyles. Modern business business enterprise leaders have to further prepare for succession, making sure that their organization can maintain growing and thrive even if they stand down.

In summary, modern-day business enterprise leaders might also furthermore gain from Genghis Khan's lengthy-time period questioning technique thru having a clear vision, taking component in strategic making plans, being bendy and adaptive, being chronic, and making geared up for succession. By enforcing the ones techniques, commercial enterprise corporation leaders can also moreover enhance the risk of lengthy-time period achievement for their organizations.

Genghis Khan's prolonged-time period thinking method had a top notch have an impact on at the development of the Mongol Empire, and his legacy is still felt in recent times. Some of the effects of his extended-time period wondering method are:

Expansion of the Mongol Empire: Genghis Khan's strategic planning and extended-time period thinking enabled him to acquire a outstanding army and conquer surrounding regions. This culminated inside the growth of the Mongol Empire to turn out to be in fact one a number of the most important empires in facts.

Cultural Exchange: Genghis Khan recommended cultural exchange and tolerance interior his u.S.A., letting humans from severa traditions stay and paintings collectively. This enabled to dissemination of thoughts and upgrades in some unspecified time within the destiny of the empire and contributed to the appearance of new era and statistics.

Administrative modifications: Genghis Khan undertook administrative modifications that helped to control the first rate areas of the

Mongol Empire. These adjustments blanketed a gain-based device for deciding on officials, a criminal code, and a uniform tool of weights and measures. These adjustments helped to assemble a more inexperienced and structured empire.

effect in Current Times: Genghis Khan's impact stays felt in present day instances. He is diagnosed as a photograph of Mongolian satisfaction and identification, and his manage tendencies and army techniques have been studied and copied thru navy commanders within the path of statistics.

In summation, Genghis Khan's prolonged-time period questioning method had a massive have an effect on at the development of the Mongol Empire, culminating in its growth and cultural interchange. His administrative innovations helped to collect a more green and based totally empire, and his impact stays felt in gift instances.

Chapter 9: Applying Genghis Khan's Leadership Strategies To Modern Business And Life

You have honestly all heard of Genghis Khan, whose call truely inspires images of a furry savage tyrant frightening and robbing the ancient globe. I'll confess I had a comparable notion till recently as soon as I got here upon a chunk of writing documenting the close to-exceptional impressiveness of his exploits.

Genghis Khan might have been cruel, unforgiving, and violent on the identical time as required, but he is a brilliant deal a whole lot much less called being one of the most smart and pragmatic commanders, tacticians, and conquerors of all time.

While the harshness and fury of his deeds need to now not be favored (and honestly aren't appropriate to the twenty first century), the ideas Genghis Khan espoused that gave begin to his triumphs are without a doubt as critical in these days's company environment. A universe that, at its center, isn't always so removed from the fierce and violent spirit of 13th-century battle.

I've tried to symbolize Genghis' most a hit manipulate strategies as a meritocracy, field, loyalty, and resolve. These 4 attributes allowed Genghis Khan to take warring bands of nomadic tribesmen and integrate them to emerge as likely the most a achievement navy in records, carving out an empire rivaled in period only with the aid of the British, some seven hundred years later.

These strategies, which added achievement to Genghis, are simply as applicable to any current management function and, whilst carried out successfully, may additionally certainly let you construct an empire of your non-public.

Meritocracy

It ought to be noted that for his time, Genghis Khan modified into as contemporary and beforehand-thinking as it receives. One of his most effective skills have emerge as his first-rate potential to discern cost in people and area them in his agency effectively.

I sincerely have few talents, therefore I am eager on smart guys, treating them as my brothers." Genghis Khan

The amazing majority of monarchs and rulers in this era built their armies and administrations spherical nepotism, cronyism, and aristocratic privilege. Genghis, however, favored competence, flair, and skills appreciably else and will surround himself with people he felt would brilliant serve the empire and its people, regardless of their origins.

Exemplifying his conviction on this, Genghis is claimed to have employed an enemy soldier who controlled to harm him with an arrow in fight. Once the combat have become concluded, Genghis asked the vanquished to confess who had shot him.

The enemy soldier, Jebe, stepped up and confessed, however he claimed to Genghis that if he stored his existence, he would in all likelihood have his famous allegiance. Genghis observed Jebe's potential and, recognizing honesty, competence, and loyalty, pardoned him and placed him interior his military, in the long run successfully ascending to come to be one of the Khan's pinnacle generals.

Today's leaders and bosses may also moreover look at in Genghis' footsteps, each through the usage of maintaining cognizant of their honestly genuinely worth and bounds and thru manner of non-discriminatorily assigning responsibilities to and elevating employees with recognized price and enjoy. Perhaps, like Genghis, even via the acquisition of employees from competing corporations?

Indeed, designing your business business enterprise in the identical manner Genghis Khan constructed his army will no longer simplest generate an inexperienced and powerful group but additionally permit man or woman flaws to be addressed with the resource of a persevering with synergy amongst personnel. This is in addition strengthened with the aid of the sturdy loyalty and area fostered in each soldier (worker).

Mongol Teamwork

Discipline and loyalty

Discipline is what enabled the Mongol military to hold itself below severe times and in some unspecified time in the future of big distances, preventing and destroying armies at the equal time as being drastically outnumbered.

The problem Genghis sanctioned end up situation to each man or woman underneath his manipulate. There were no particular privileges for generals or commanders. In fact, if a super lost a struggle or an officer made a sizeable enough mistakes, he'd be decreased to the popularity of a ordinary soldier.

While the schooling became tough and demanding, it turned into in no way immoderate or unduly immoderate. Genghis ensured that his warriors have been taught about as many scenarios as they'll envision, stressing schooling.

Discipline and arrangements in conflict are sincerely as critical as steerage in industrial organization. A nicely-informed person is appreciably more a hit and treasured and is plenty much less possibly to have gaps in their running skills.

Much like Genghis' military, a successful schooling utility not handiest enhances ordinary usual overall performance however additionally forges loyalty and fosters a experience of collective cohesion among employees.

Genghis became likewise adverse to micromanagement, usually leaving his officials and commanders liberty in how they trained and controlled their warriors, so long as the more dreams have been happy.

Where this technique helped the Mongols avoid the common faults of a completely strict control device, it's miles just as treasured when walking your agency. It has been set up that micromanaging at any business enterprise diploma might also produce an array of terrible effects, which incorporates distrust, lack of loyalty, reduced morale, excessively reliant humans, and reduced productiveness, to mention a few.

Genghis have become stated to encourage loyalty in numerous strategies, considered considered certainly one of which, you'll agree, resembles a present day-day worker incentive plan. Yes, every soldier in the Mongolian military earned a part of anything treasure turn out to be captured. Thereby selling efficiency and productiveness (at least while it came to preventing).

This very a whole lot parallels cutting-edge worker percentage schemes, with many groups have found out the blessings of such an method. Rewarding employees after the employer has had a robust economic 12 months aligns worker pursuits with those of the enterprise and might bring about a massive boost in productiveness, loyalty, and engagement.

Determination

Genghis Khan very masses led with the useful resource of example. His unmatched dedication and sheer stress of may have an impact on all those who decided him.

"There isn't any price in some detail until it is completed." Genghis Khan

There had been few men in records with this form of solve to gain their goals or even fewer who've finished it.

Having imaginative and prescient, choice, and resolution are definitely the maximum critical attributes of any leader. Genghis stimulated his troops to have a look at him. His story is corresponding to that of a poetry or epic tale: Genghis Khan ascended from modest roots to become the conqueror of the seemed international. An accomplishment found out through his unshakeable motive of a unified worldwide.

While dedication is vital to fulfillment in masses of sectors of existence, it's miles specially applicable to growing a enterprise enterprise and being a leader in such respects.

"There are many moments which can be complete of depression and soreness when you have to fireside people and cancel topics and cope with very difficult situations... It's so tough (to construct a organization) that in case you don't have a passion, you'll surrender."

Steve Jobs, CEO of Apple Inc.

Having pressure, willpower, and imaginative and prescient lets in transformation. They are the unquestionable pillars of fulfillment. It is the first-rate maintaining those skills who doesn't give up while the going receives hard and who continues pushing till they reap. Determination normal Genghis' empire; will it forge yours too?

I choice this post offers a chunk perception into the genius of Genghis Khan and the way he may moreover have an effect on your business enterprise techniques and your private lifestyles. I invite you to adopt your have a look at and discover more about this interesting conqueror.

Chapter 10: Early Life

Genghis Khan's early life modified into marked with the useful resource of hassle and conflict. Born right right into a circle of relatives of nomadic herders, he placed out the techniques of the steppe at an early age. He end up really nine years antique whilst his father became poisoned via the usage of a rival extended own family, leaving him and his own family inclined and without safety.

In the years that placed, Genghis Khan and his circle of relatives were compelled to fend for themselves, living off the land and preventing off rival clans. It have turn out to be at some stage in this time that Genghis Khan developed the survival talents that would serve him properly inside the course of his life.

Despite the demanding situations he faced, Genghis Khan remained determined and innovative. He fashioned alliances with exceptional tribes and decided the artwork of negotiation, competencies that could later assist him unite the Mongol tribes and forge a effective empire.

It wasn't till his late teens that Genghis Khan began to turn out to be a frontrunner in his very private right. He led a a success raid in opposition to a rival tribe, incomes him the respect and admiration of his friends. With every subsequent victory, Genghis Khan's legend grew, and he began out to draw fans from throughout the Mongol steppes.

By the time he become in his thirties, Genghis Khan had emerged because the undisputed chief of the Mongols, with a popularity as a fierce warrior and extremely good strategist. It changed into then that he began out to expose his interest to conquest, embarking on a series of campaigns that could deliver him to the heights of power and go away an indelible mark on international data.

As a younger boy, Genghis Khan end up stated for his quiet and introspective nature. He spent lots of his time on my own, looking at the area spherical him and contemplating his place in it. It modified into at some stage in the ones solitary moments that he commenced to broaden the intellectual interest and introspection that could set him aside from different leaders of his time.

Despite his introspective nature, Genghis Khan changed into moreover acknowledged for his physical prowess and bravado. He have turn out to be an finished horseman and expert with a bow and arrow, talents that he honed via years of practice and training. His physical energy and martial prowess could serve him nicely all through his existence, permitting him to steer his armies into battle and emerge positive in opposition to even the maximum ambitious foes.

Despite his many successes, Genghis Khan never forgot his humble roots. He remained deeply associated with his people and the land that had fashioned him, and he never disregarded the values that had sustained him within the route of his existence. It changed into this deep connection to his humans and his history that made him this sort of favored and respected leader, and that would make certain his enduring legacy for hundreds of destiny years back.

Rise to Power

As a extra youthful guy, Genghis Khan had already set up himself as a leader amongst his human beings, manner to his army successes and his smart political acumen. However, it wasn't until he united the Mongol tribes under his banner that he surely began to emerge as a powerful determine.

Genghis Khan's rise to power have become a slow one, marked by means of a sequence of alliances and betrayals. He fashioned close to relationships with extraordinary effective leaders, inclusive of his early life pal Jamuka, but in the long run broke with them while their hobbies diverged.

It have become throughout his advertising campaign against the Tatars that Genghis Khan in reality started out to emerge as a navy leader of the number one rank. He led his forces with capacity and cunning, sudden his enemies along with his unconventional methods and his lightning-speedy raids. By the time the advertising marketing campaign changed into over, Genghis Khan had established himself as a force to be reckoned with, and his recognition satisfactory grew with every subsequent victory.

As he conquered increasingly territory, Genghis Khan became an increasing number of assured and bold. He commenced to look himself as greater than most effective a tribal leader, however as a ruler with the electricity to form the future of his humans. And it grow to be this ambition that could in the end lead him to overcome massive swathes of territory and installation one of the most effective empires in facts.

As Genghis Khan persisted to make bigger his empire, he faced severa worrying conditions from each internal and outside property. One of the largest worrying situations he faced become from the Khwarazmian Empire, a effective u . S . A . That managed lots of Central Asia.

In 1219, Genghis Khan launched a large invasion of the Khwarazmian Empire, looking for to amplify his territory and consolidate his energy. The invasion modified into marked via a series of brutal battles, wherein Genghis Khan's forces emerged a hit way to their advanced techniques and navy place.

Despite going thru overwhelming odds, Genghis Khan refused to back down or compromise. He have grow to be decided to win the least bit charges, although it supposed sacrificing his very own guys. This ruthless dedication earned him a fearsome reputation, and his enemies quick determined out to fear his wrath.

Over the following few years, Genghis Khan endured to triumph over new territories, from China inside the east to Russia in the west. His empire stretched from the Pacific Ocean to the Caspian Sea, and he emerge as broadly seemed as one of the quality and influential leaders inside the global.

Despite his many accomplishments, Genghis Khan remained humble and proper to his roots. He endured to live a easy lifestyles, frequently sleeping in a tent and ingesting on clean food of meat and milk. And he in no way forgot the values that had sustained him at some point of his existence, values like loyalty, braveness, and perseverance. It have become those values that made him the form of cherished and respected chief, and that ensured his enduring legacy for loads of future years returned.

Genghis Khan changed into born right right into a terrible own family in the harsh and unforgiving environment of the Mongolian steppes. From a younger age, he became compelled to fend for himself, looking and herding in case you want to stay on. But even as a more youthful boy, he showed fantastic intelligence and resourcefulness, in addition to a fierce self-control to succeed.

As he grew older, Genghis Khan began out to make a call for himself as a warrior and a leader. He prominent himself in conflict, prevailing the respect and admiration of his fellow tribesmen. And he validated a eager facts of politics, forging alliances and constructing networks of help that could show beneficial in his later campaigns.

In his early thirties, Genghis Khan began out to turn out to be a extreme contender for electricity. He had already installation himself because the leader of his very very own tribe, and he started to reap out to exclusive tribes, searching out to form alliances and consolidate his function.

One of his maximum essential early allies come to be Jamuka, a kids pal and fellow warrior. Together, the two men waged battle toward their enemies, grade by grade gaining increasingly more territory and feature an impact on. But as their power grew, so too did their goals, and finally their friendship started out to get to the bottom of.

In a bitter and continual conflict, Genghis Khan and Jamuka faced off in competition to every distinct for control of the Mongol tribes. It turn out to be a brutal and bloody warfare, marked with the aid of treachery, betrayal, and the wholesale slaughter of tens of masses of humans. But in the long run, it changed into Genghis Khan who emerged powerful, thanks in no small element to his army genius and his unwavering power of will.

With his competition vanquished, Genghis Khan have come to be free to pursue his imaginative and prescient of a unified Mongol country. He launched into a series of campaigns in competition to neighboring tribes and kingdoms, grade by grade increasing his territory and consolidating his power. And as he conquered increasingly land, his popularity as a warrior and a pacesetter grew, until he became widely seemed as one of the maximum effective guys within the international.

But even as he basked in the glow of his many triumphs, Genghis Khan by no means forgot his humble beginnings. He remained grounded and centered on his desires, typically striving to decorate himself and his human beings. And it end up this unshakable willpower and unwavering willpower to his motive that might in the end lead him to end up one of the finest conquerors in data.

Chapter 11: Military Tactics And Conquests

Genghis Khan modified right into a grasp strategist and a top notch army commander. He become famend for his ability to out-count on and outmaneuver his warring parties, and for his ruthless willpower to win in any respect charges.

One of Genghis Khan's key navy tactics have become his use of a specially mobile cavalry pressure. He recognized that the large, open steppes of Mongolia furnished ideal situations for instant-shifting horsemen, and he worked tirelessly to create a disciplined and effective cavalry stress that could enjoy suddenly and strike tough.

Another of Genghis Khan's methods changed into his ability to comply to changing instances on the battlefield. He turned into not wedded to any unique method or plan of assault, but changed into as an opportunity constantly seeking out methods to outflank and outmaneuver his warring parties. This flexibility and adaptability made him a effective opponent, and helped him to accumulate victory in masses of tough battles.

Perhaps one of the maximum debatable additives of Genghis Khan's army campaigns was his use of terror and brutality as a way of intimidating his enemies. He have become acknowledged to order the wholesale slaughter of complete populations, and to apply captured prisoners as human shields or to launch human wave attacks in opposition to fortified positions. While those techniques have been in reality powerful in cowing his fighters, additionally they left a direction of devastation and horror of their wake.

Another controversial detail of Genghis Khan's army campaigns is the volume to which he depended on distant places troops and mercenaries. Some historians have speculated that as hundreds as 1/2 of

Genghis Khan's army also can furthermore have been made of non-Mongol combatants, collectively with Turks, Uighurs, or maybe Europeans. While this allowed him to issue a greater severa and effective military, it additionally raised questions about his dedication to his non-public humans and his willingness to rely on outsiders to reap his desires.

Despite those controversies and speculations, there may be no question that Genghis Khan's army conquests had been the numerous most sudden in human history. He conquered large swathes of territory, together with a whole lot of China, Central Asia, and Eastern Europe. And he did so with a pace and performance that become unequalled through every other conqueror earlier than or for the cause that.

But perhaps maximum incredible of all come to be Genghis Khan's potential to unite the disparate tribes and factions of Mongolia right proper right into a single, cohesive country. He diagnosed that his people can be extra effective collectively than they ever may be aside, and he labored tirelessly to construct bridges and forge alliances between wonderful companies. In the give up, it modified into this unifying imaginative and prescient that allowed him to create one of the best empires the vicinity has ever seen.

Genghis Khan's conquests started out within the early thirteenth century at the identical time as he modified into still in his 20s. At that factor, Mongolia emerge as a patchwork of rival tribes and clans, every with their personal traditions and loyalties. Genghis Khan diagnosed that if he preferred to unite these tribes and create a powerful new country, he could likely need to do away with his warring parties and consolidate his energy.

To achieve this, Genghis Khan started a chain of military campaigns in opposition to his pals. He have emerge as a outstanding tactician, and he used his cavalry to remarkable impact, the usage of lightning-speedy maneuvers to outflank and crush his enemies. In war after conflict, he defeated rival chieftains and their armies, frequently building his private strength base and consolidating his control over the vicinity.

As Genghis Khan's energy grew, he set his attractions on new conquests. In 1211, he led his army into the Jin Empire, which controlled numerous northern China. The Jin were a effective foe, with a big, nicely-professional navy and complicated fortifications. But Genghis Khan grow to be undaunted, and he released a chain of devastating assaults on Jin towns and cities, laying waste to the geographical area and sowing worry and panic some of the close by population.

Over the course of severa years, Genghis Khan's armies steadily wore down the Jin Empire, shooting key cities and fortresses and bringing an awful lot of northern China beneath their manipulate. In 1215, Genghis Khan declared himself Emperor of the Great Mongol Nation, and he persisted his campaigns of conquest in the course of the rest of his lifestyles.

Genghis Khan's conquests were now not limited to China, however. He moreover have become his interest to Central Asia, in which he defeated the powerful Khwarezmian Empire and set up Mongol manipulate over a whole lot of the place. He then released campaigns into Russia and Eastern Europe, defeating the Kievan Rus and awesome community rulers and developing a massive Mongol Empire that stretched from the Pacific Ocean to the Black Sea.

Throughout his conquests, Genghis Khan became ruthless and unrelenting. He confirmed little mercy to people who antagonistic him, and he changed into mentioned to order the wholesale slaughter of whole populations. But he modified into moreover a brilliant organizer and chief, who recognized the significance of preserving his troops well-fed and well-prepared, and of using worldwide circle of relatives individuals and alliances to enhance his position.

In the end, Genghis Khan's conquests converted the political landscape of tons of Asia and Europe. He created a sizable empire that added collectively human beings of different cultures and traditions, and he laid the inspiration for a today's technology of alternate and trade that would in the end be a part of the whole worldwide. And even as his techniques can also have been brutal, there can be no denying the impact that he had on the path of human information.

1206: Genghis Khan will become the pleasant leader of the Mongol tribes.

1207-1210: Genghis Khan launches a series of campaigns towards neighboring tribes to consolidate his strength in Mongolia.

1211-1215: Genghis Khan leads his armies into northern China and starts offevolved offevolved his conquest of the Jin Empire.

1219-1221: Genghis Khan launches a advertising and marketing campaign in the direction of the Khwarezmian Empire in Central Asia, defeating them and establishing Mongol control over the region.

1223: Genghis Khan defeats a coalition of Russian princes at the Battle of Kalka River.

1227: Genghis Khan dies whilst campaigning in competition to the Western Xia Empire in northern China.

Conquering an military of hundreds is straightforward, but conquering your self is the genuine conquest."

The satisfactory victory is that which calls for no conflict."

I am the sword of the kingdom. When the state desires a sword, I unsheathe it. When the kingdom not goals it, I sheathe it."

A chief leads through using way of example, not via pressure."

I do not worry an navy of lions led by using a sheep; I worry an navy of sheep led with the aid of a lion."

I have conquered lands and those not with the aid of using strain, but via the use of harmony. I unite people below the banner of the Mongol usa, and that they grow to be invincible."

It is not sufficient to overcome; one need to furthermore understand a way to rule."

The energy of a wall is neither more nor an entire lot a great deal less than the braveness of those who guard it."

Do not appearance down on a susceptible opponent, for even a fly can cause a lion to fall."

Chapter 12: Impact On Mongol Culture

Genghis Khan now not first-rate left behind a legacy of navy conquests, however also a profound effect on Mongol culture that still reverberates to at the moment. Under his manipulate, the Mongols skilled a cultural renaissance that transformed their way of existence and created a long lasting legacy that also endures.

One of the maximum massive cultural modifications added about through using Genghis Khan have become the adoption of a written language. Prior to his reign, the Mongols had no written script and trusted an oral lifestyle to keep their records and way of lifestyles. Genghis Khan recognized the significance of recording his achievements and developing a written language to unite his people. He commissioned college college students to extend a writing tool based mostly on the Uighur script, which ultimately brought approximately the appearance of the

Mongolian script this is despite the fact that used in recent times.

In addition to his contributions to written language, Genghis Khan additionally achieved a feature in shaping Mongol traditions and customs. He carried out a prison code, the Yassa, which supplied a framework for social agency and justice. The Yassa codified tips of conduct, belongings rights, and governance, and became a excessive step forward in putting in place a unified Mongol identification.

Furthermore, Genghis Khan's impact on Mongol way of life extended past his reign. The Mongols persisted to unfold their way of existence and traditions throughout the large territories they conquered, leaving at the back of lasting legacies in places like China, Central Asia, and Eastern Europe. For instance, in China, Mongol rule brought about the improvement of the Forbidden City and exceptional great architectural achievements that also stand to these days.

Even in present day instances, Genghis Khan's have an impact on on Mongol way of lifestyles remains strong. His photograph ornaments forex, stamps, and different national symbols, and his legacy is widely known in Mongolian folklore and song. His contributions to Mongol way of life are a testomony to his enduring legacy as a frontrunner who converted his humans and left a long lasting mark on data.

Genghis Khan's have an effect on on Mongol tradition have become no longer constrained to language, regulation, and governance. He moreover played a big position in shaping Mongol art work and faith. Under his reign, the Mongols advanced a completely unique style of paintings that protected traditional designs and motifs with factors from one-of-a-kind cultures they encountered at some point of their conquests. This delivered approximately a extremely good fusion of styles this is no matter the fact that diagnosed and well-known these days.

Genghis Khan's religious views have been moreover a super have an impact on on Mongol way of lifestyles. While he himself turn out to be not non secular, he recognized the significance of religion in uniting his human beings and setting up a shared set of values. He recommended the exercise of Shamanism, which was the conventional religion of the Mongols, and furthermore supported other religions which incorporates Buddhism, Christianity, and Islam. This religious tolerance become a marked departure from the intolerance and persecution that characterised many one-of-a-kind empires of the time.

Genghis Khan's effect on Mongol manner of life moreover extended to their cuisine and fashion. Under his rule, the Mongols accompanied new substances and cooking strategies from the severa cultures they encountered. For instance, using spices and herbs in cooking changed into brought to the Mongols with the beneficial useful resource of the Persians and feature grow to be a staple in Mongolian delicacies. Similarly, Genghis Khan's army campaigns added him into contact with one-of-a-kind kinds of clothing and armor, which stimulated adjustments in Mongol fashion.

In current-day instances, Genghis Khan's legacy keeps to encourage Mongolians to have a laugh their manner of lifestyles and historical past. For example, in Mongolia's capital city of Ulaanbaatar, a massive statue of Genghis Khan stands as a photo of the dominion's information and satisfaction. The statue, this is considered one of the largest equestrian statues within the global, is a well-known traveller appeal and a supply of national identification.

Overall, Genghis Khan's impact on Mongol manner of existence became an prolonged manner-achieving and transformative. His contributions to language, regulation, artwork, religion, delicacies, and fashion helped to form the Mongol identity and left a protracted lasting legacy that also resonates to these days.

Language:

Genghis Khan diagnosed the significance of language as a way of verbal exchange and governance. Under his rule, Mongol became the expert language of the empire, and he set up a written language device based totally totally on the Uyghur script. He moreover promoted the use of different languages, in conjunction with Chinese, Persian, and Arabic, that permits you to facilitate alternate and global individuals of the family with neighboring regions.

Law and Governance:

Genghis Khan's impact on Mongol regulation and governance changed into massive. He mounted a centralized system of presidency that turned into primarily based mostly on a strict code of criminal tips referred to as the Yasa. The Yasa set up policies for the whole thing from inheritance and belongings rights to navy company and exchange. It moreover supplied for a system of justice that changed into honest and equitable, and it helped to sell social and economic stability at some stage in the empire.

Art:

Genghis Khan's effect on Mongol paintings was profound. He advocated the improvement of a totally unique fashion that covered traditional designs and motifs with factors from one among a type cultures. This fusion of patterns resulted in a one-of-a-kind Mongol paintings that is nonetheless diagnosed and well-known nowadays. Examples of Mongol paintings from this era embody decorative metalwork, ceramics, textiles, and portray.

Religion:

Genghis Khan's non secular views have been a huge have an effect on on Mongol manner of life. Although he end up not non secular himself, he identified the importance of religion in unifying his humans and promoting a shared set of values. He recommended the workout of Shamanism, that have emerge as the traditional faith of the Mongols. He furthermore supported other religions, together with Buddhism, Christianity, and Islam, and allowed for the unfastened exercising of faith at some stage inside the empire. This religious tolerance end up a marked departure from the intolerance and persecution that characterised many precise empires of the time.

Cuisine:

Genghis Khan's impact on Mongol cuisine changed into moreover huge. His military campaigns delivered him into contact with new meals and cooking strategies from the diverse cultures he encountered. This added at the adoption of latest elements and cooking techniques, collectively with using spices and herbs, which have been delivered to the Mongols thru the Persians. Mongolian cuisine in recent times shows this fusion of styles and flavors, and includes dishes which embody buuz (steamed dumplings), khuushuur (deep-fried pastries), and tsuivan (stir-fried noodles).

Fashion:

Genghis Khan's impact on Mongol style become moreover incredible. His military campaigns added him into contact with one-of-a-kind types of clothing and armor, which stimulated changes in Mongol fashion. For example, the advent of chainmail armor from Persia brought approximately the development of the deel, a conventional Mongol gown that changed into designed to be worn over chainmail. The deel stays a well-known item of apparel in Mongolia in recent times.

Chapter 13: The Silk Road

Genghis Khan's conquests now not most effective expanded the Mongol Empire, however furthermore facilitated the hollow of the well-known Silk Road. The Silk Road changed into a community of change routes that connected the East and West, bearing in mind the exchange of products, ideas, and cultures. This path facilitated the change of silk, spices, tea, porcelain, and lots of numerous treasured commodities.

Genghis Khan recognized the importance of change in keeping the wealth and balance of his empire. He recommended the secure passage of investors and traders along the Silk Road, and ensured that they have been protected from bandits and thieves. As a cease end result, the Silk Road flourished under his rule and became a key factor inside the financial increase of the empire.

The Silk Road furthermore served as a channel for the alternate of thoughts and information some of the East and West. It facilitated the spread of religions at the side of Buddhism, Christianity, and Islam, in addition to the change of clinical and philosophical thoughts. The know-how and generation of papermaking, printing, and gunpowder had been furthermore disseminated alongside the Silk Road.

Even nowadays, the legacy of the Silk Road endures. It maintains to serve as a photo of the interconnectedness of the location, and the significance of change and cultural alternate. The cities that when thrived along the Silk Road, which encompass Samarkand and Kashgar, although bear witness to the effect of Genghis Khan and the Mongol Empire.

In end, Genghis Khan's effect on the Silk Road modified into massive. He no longer best facilitated the hole of the exchange course, however additionally identified the significance of change and cultural trade for the growth of his empire. His legacy continues to undergo nowadays, because the Silk Road serves as a testament to the interconnectedness of the area and the importance of world change and cultural trade.

The Silk Road, a mythical exchange course that stretched over four,000 miles from China to the Mediterranean, holds an air of mystique and intrigue. It come to be a community of interconnected routes that enabled the alternate of products, thoughts, and lifestyle amongst East and West. And on the coronary coronary heart of this historical trade route stood Genghis Khan and his empire.

Under Genghis Khan's rule, the Silk Road have turn out to be a bustling hub of alternate, connecting the nomadic peoples of the steppes with the greater settled civilizations of China, India, Persia, and Europe. The Khan's armies blanketed the investors and investors who journeyed alongside the Silk Road, and his government regulated alternate and exchange, making sure secure passage and sincere charges for all.

But there was extra to the Silk Road than sincerely exchange. It modified into furthermore a conduit for mind, faith, and manner of existence. Buddhism, Islam, and Christianity all spread alongside the Silk Road, as did advances in era, remedy, and the arts. Genghis Khan's empire, with its multicultural populace and tolerant mind-set closer to variety, played a vital role in fostering this trade of data and lifestyle. Yet, notwithstanding its importance, the Silk Road moreover held many mysteries and secrets and techniques and techniques and strategies. It become a place of hazard and adventure, in which travelers braved harsh climates, treacherous terrain, and the threat of bandits and raiders. And some say that the Silk Road have become additionally a hotbed of espionage and intrigue, in which spies and dealers from superb empires vied for strength and feature an effect on.

All in all, the Silk Road was a essential part of Genghis Khan's legacy, one which unique the path of statistics and left an extended-lasting effect on the area. The Silk Road was now not best a bodily exchange route, but it moreover facilitated the alternate of know-how, thoughts, and cultures. Genghis Khan recognized the importance of this route and sought to govern it, ensuring the protection of the shoppers and the caravans that traveled it. The Mongol Empire's big territory allowed for a free go with the flow of merchandise and thoughts, and the Silk Road have grow to be a melting pot of cultures, religions, and technology.

The Mongol Empire's manipulate of the Silk Road brought at the unfold of improvements along with paper money, the compass, and gunpowder to Europe, that might later cause the Renaissance. It moreover facilitated the alternate of mind among one-of-a-type civilizations, critical to the development of latest techniques in medicine, astronomy, and arithmetic. The Silk Road become no longer simplest a hub for financial interest, but it moreover accomplished a sizable feature within the improvement of human civilization.

However, the Silk Road also had its darker side. Alongside the buyers came the unfold of ailment, which includes the infamous Black Death. The Silk Road modified into additionally utilized by criminals and bandits to smuggle items and those for the duration of borders, making it a unstable location to journey.

Despite its traumatic conditions, the Silk Road remained an crucial exchange course for masses of years until it have emerge as in the end modified by using the usage of the use of sea routes after the invention of the New World. Its effect on global statistics and way of life can't be overstated, and its legacy lives on in the many cultural and technological exchanges that happened alongside its route.

According to 3 estimates, the Silk Road stretched over 6,000 kilometers and concerned the motion of merchandise and mind among China, India, Persia, and Europe. It facilitated the exchange of products which embody silk, tea, spices, and specific high-priced devices. The alternate alongside the Silk Road have emerge as not actually constrained to gadgets, as mind, philosophies, and religions moreover flowed along its routes.

Genghis Khan's conquests and enlargement of the Mongol Empire had a first-rate effect on the Silk Road. The Mongol Empire created a huge and regular community of exchange routes, making it an awful lot less complicated and more secure for merchants to tour across the continent. The Mongols additionally promoted the use of paper foreign exchange, which facilitated trade and change. It is expected that in the Mongol generation, the quantity of alternate along the Silk Road accelerated tenfold.

Furthermore, Genghis Khan's have an impact on on the Silk Road prolonged beyond exchange and commerce. His empire become a cultural melting pot that added together human beings from numerous backgrounds and ideals. The trade of thoughts and philosophies led to a skip-pollination of cultures that enriched the area's artwork, track, and literature. It is concept that the famous card challenge of "pai gow" originated from the Mongol Empire and made its way to China through the Silk Road.

Today, the impact of Genghis Khan and the Silk Road can but be felt in lots of components of the arena. The Silk Road has come to be a popular vacationer excursion spot, and many countries alongside its routes have preserved its historic net websites and cultural traditions. The Mongol Empire's legacy is likewise obvious in the cuisines, music, and art work of many nations, together with Mongolia, China, and Central Asia. The effect of the Silk Road and Genghis Khan on worldwide facts and manner of lifestyles cannot be overstated.

Political and Social Legacy

Genghis Khan's political and social legacy is easy. He installation a device of presidency that modified into based totally totally on meritocracy, in location of hereditary fame. This supposed that everybody who confirmed know-how or potential need to rise up inside the ranks of society, regardless of their history or upbringing. This become a modern-day idea in a time on the identical time as birthright and circle of relatives connections have been the whole lot.

Under Genghis Khan's rule, the Mongol Empire grew to turn out to be the most important contiguous empire in data. This enlargement introduced approximately a cultural change, in which tremendous people from one-of-a-type areas had been uncovered to new thoughts and customs. It also allowed for the dissemination of knowledge and innovations, which had an extended-lasting impact on the sector.

One of the most brilliant legacies of Genghis Khan's reign became the Pax Mongolica, a period of relative peace and stability that lasted for over a century. This changed into completed thru the arrival of a excellent community of exchange routes, along with the famous Silk Road, which facilitated the exchange of products and mind for the duration of Asia and Europe. The secure passage of investors and buyers turned into ensured with the resource of the Mongol Empire's navy may additionally, which acted as a deterrent to banditry and piracy.

Genghis Khan's have an effect on can nonetheless be felt in contemporary-day instances. He is regarded as a hero in Mongolia and different elements of Central

Asia, wherein his legacy is well known through statues, monuments, and different types of cultural expression. His impact on the sector is likewise apparent in the severa loanwords which have entered the English language, on the side of "yurt," "khan," and "steppe."

As you can see, Genghis Khan's political and social legacy is rich and varied, and continues to be felt in particular factors of the place nowadays. Despite the substantial empire that Genghis Khan created, his legacy moreover had a dark side. His brutal strategies in warfare and the subjugation of conquered peoples left an extended-lasting effect on the political and social systems of the regions he conquered. The Khan's armies had been seemed for their ferocity, and they will regularly appoint strategies which incorporates decimation, the practice of killing each 10th individual in a captured town or city as a shape of punishment.

Furthermore, Genghis Khan's regulations of forced assimilation and suppression of close by customs and traditions induced widespread suffering for the conquered peoples. The Khan's reign become marked thru the enslavement and forced migration of loads of lots of people, main to the deaths of limitless others because of starvation, sickness, and violence.

Even in the present day, the effects of Genghis Khan's legacy can though be felt. The political and social structures of many areas of Asia are regardless of the reality that long-installed through the Khan's empire, and the Mongol conquests had been stated as one of the most big motives of the spread of the bubonic plague. It is predicted that the Khan's campaigns brought approximately the deaths of as tons as 40 million humans, accounting for as masses as 10% of the world's populace on the time.

The impact of Genghis Khan's legacy additionally may be visible within the upward thrust of nationalist and extremist moves in present day instances, with agencies mentioning his brutal approaches and techniques as justification for their non-public violent movements. The Khan's lasting effect on the arena is a testomony to the electricity and unfavourable nature of conquest and the importance of facts the legacy of ancient figures, each precise and lousy.

Despite the awful recognition that Genghis Khan has obtained over the years, it is honestly well worth noting that he wasn't all doom and gloom. In reality, he had quite the humorousness. There's a tale this is going that after, after a specially gruesome conflict, Genghis and his troops had been feasting on a freshly slaughtered goat. When a person asked him what he idea of the meal, Genghis spoke back with a grin, "I determine upon my goat medium unusual, however this one seems a touch on the well-completed issue."

But on a more important word, Genghis Khan's political and social legacy is apparent. His creation of the Mongol Empire paved the manner for a ultra-modern era of alternate and trade, and his policies of non secular tolerance and gain-primarily based totally merchandising helped to interrupt down the constraints amongst one in every of a kind cultures and ethnicities. The outcomes of his rule can though be felt in loads of additives of the arena these days, and it's miles smooth that Genghis Khan's impact is probably felt for lots generations to come back.

Despite the ones humorous anecdotes, there may be no question that Genghis Khan's political and social legacy has had an enduring effect on the arena. His fame quo of a centralized authorities and prison device laid the inspiration for the Mongol Empire's prolonged-lasting fulfillment.

Additionally, his advertising and marketing of religious tolerance and cultural change set a precedent for future rulers and empires to observe.

Moreover, Genghis Khan's legacy may be visible within the present-day Mongolian way of existence and society. In Mongolia, he is nicely called a countrywide hero and his photograph is featured on the u . S .'s forex. The Mongolian human beings additionally keep to exercising the numerous customs and traditions that have been set up at some point of the time of the Mongol Empire.

Outside of Mongolia, Genghis Khan's legacy has moreover left a mark on worldwide lifestyle. From well-known films and books to the usage of the term "Mongol Horde" to offer an reason for a massive, effective enterprise, Genghis Khan's have an effect on can despite the fact that be felt nowadays.

In cease, Genghis Khan modified right into a complicated historic determine whose effect on the sector can not be overstated. From his youngsters as a nomadic warrior to his upward thrust because the chief of one in every of the most important empires in statistics, his story is one which continues to fascinate and intrigue humans to in the mean time. His legacy as a military strategist, political chief, and cultural icon has left an indelible mark on global information and will stay studied and noted for generations to come again.

Chapter 14: Legacy In Modern Times

As the centuries handed, Genghis Khan's legacy endured to solid a protracted shadow over the arena. Some historians argue that his effect at the present day global is even more than that of another historic discern. In the phrases of Dan Brown, "Genghis Khan's impact can be visible in the entirety from global politics to popular subculture, from the halls of strength to the darkest corners of the internet."

Despite his recognition as a conqueror, Genghis Khan's proper legacy lies now not inside the destruction he wrought, but in the manner of existence he created. His empire changed into one of the most cosmopolitan and severa in statistics, encompassing human beings of all races, religions, and backgrounds. Under his management, the Mongols have emerge as one of the most tolerant and open-minded societies of their time, with a strong emphasis on meritocracy and identical opportunity.

Today, Genghis Khan's legacy lives on in myriad strategies. His navy procedures and techniques keep to inspire current military leaders, on the identical time as his mind approximately governance and control maintain to form political discourse spherical the arena. In the arena of popular lifestyle, he has been immortalized in endless movies, books, and video video video games, from the traditional 1956 movie "The Conqueror" to the greater modern day "Age of Empires II: The Conquerors" increase p.C..

But probable the maximum unexpected legacy of Genghis Khan is his impact on current genetics. Recent studies have confirmed that as many as sixteen million humans round the arena are direct descendants of the wonderful Khan, making him one of the most prolific fathers in facts. In a worldwide in which we're continuously reminded of our versions, Genghis Khan's legacy is a effective reminder of the shared history that unites us all.

Indeed, Genghis Khan's legacy can be visible in many current-day additives of Mongolian society. His have an impact on may be visible inside the u.S.'s flag, which capabilities the soyombo image that he used as his private seal. The soyombo photo represents the group spirit of the 4 elements - earth, water, hearth, and air - and is a super function in Mongolian paintings, structure, or perhaps on their overseas cash.

In addition to this, Genghis Khan's legacy has been embraced via the Mongolian government as a supply of country wide pride. The the us of america celebrates his birthday as a country wide vacation, and masses of houses and monuments have been erected in his honor. His legacy has additionally been the state of affairs of severa books, films, and TV shows, every in Mongolia and round the sector.

Furthermore, Genghis Khan's effect can be visible beyond Mongolia's borders. His conquests and empire-constructing paved the manner for the spread of the Mongol way of lifestyles and language, further to the fame quo of the Silk Road trade network that related the East and the West. The Mongol Empire moreover had a huge impact on the improvement of worldwide family participants and worldwide members of the family, putting precedents which might be however used these days.

As it seems, Genghis Khan's legacy has even seeped into the world of leisure. In fact, some have speculated that he is the inspiration behind the notorious Dothraki horde in Game of Thrones. With their warlike lifestyle and nomadic manner of existence, it is now not difficult to see the similarities. But it truely is not all. Genghis Khan has additionally inspired an entire variety of merchandise, from t-shirts to motion figures. Who could not need a miniature Genghis Khan on their table, entire with tiny sword and conqueror's scowl?

And allow's no longer neglect approximately the Genghis Khan-themed eating places that have popped up in severa additives of the arena. Yes, you heard that right. You can now dine inside the fashion of a Mongol warrior, with dishes like "Warrior's Delight" and "Horseman's Platter" at the menu. Who is aware of, perhaps they may even serve up a component of kumis, the fermented mare's milk that became a favorite of Genghis himself.

All joking apart, it is smooth that Genghis Khan's legacy is alive and well within the modern international. From information books to famous subculture, he maintains to fascinate and intrigue us centuries after his loss of existence.

In cease, Genghis Khan's legacy stays felt in current instances, no longer best in Mongolia but additionally globally. His effect on way of life, language, and alternate, in addition to his impact on worldwide circle of relatives participants, make him one of the maximum widespread figures in worldwide records. His tale is a reminder of the strength of one character to form the route of statistics, and his legacy serves as an idea to many even these days.

Legends and Myths

As Genghis Khan's empire improved, so did the testimonies and legends surrounding him. Tales of his bravery and foxy unfold some distance and significant, charming the imaginations of people in the course of the land. But with extremely good power additionally came awesome duty, and Khan knew that his legacy may also want to boom far past his very very own lifetime.

In the midst of his army conquests, Genghis Khan positioned time to popularity on the schooling and enlightenment of his humans. He set up a gadget of prison suggestions and regulations that ensured justice and equality for all, irrespective of their social reputation or records. His cutting-edge thoughts approximately governance and social agency laid the muse for modern-day-day democracy and inspired generations of leaders to return back.

But possibly most exciting of all were the rumors that swirled round Genghis Khan's supposed magical powers. Some claimed that he should manipulate the factors themselves, summoning lightning and thunder at will. Others whispered of a thriller order of warriors, skilled within the dark arts and sworn to do his bidding.

Despite the passage of centuries, the legend of Genghis Khan endures. From Hollywood blockbusters to famous video video video games, his tale maintains to captivate and inspire. And for folks that dare to delve deeper into the mysteries surrounding this enigmatic decide, there may additionally additionally but be secrets and techniques and strategies ready to be exposed...

As the vacationers continued their adventure alongside the path of the Silk Road, they encountered various cities and towns wherein the trade of merchandise and cultures become at its top. The traders may additionally forestall and wonder on the difficult structure and bustling marketplaces that have been found in the ones cities. They observed the fusion of numerous cultures, religions, and traditions which made every area particular in its own manner.

One such town turned into Samarkand, a metropolis positioned in current-day Uzbekistan. It became regarded for its lovely mosques, madrasas, and mausoleums. The metropolis changed into additionally well-known for its silk production, which made it a amazing trading middle at the Silk Road. The tourists ought to often listen memories of the legendary ruler, Timur, who had conquered Samarkand and made it his capital within the 14th century. As they approached the metropolis, the vacationers have been in awe of the super systems that greeted them. The Registan, a grand public square, end up decorated with three madrasas that had been built inside the 15th and 17th centuries. The hard mosaics and tilework on the walls and domes of the homes had been a testomony to the imaginative and architectural achievements of the Timurid generation.

The vacationers wandered through the slender alleys of the town, taking in the sights and sounds of the bustling markets. They visited the Bibi-Khanym Mosque, one in every of the most critical mosques in Central Asia, constructed thru Timur himself inside the 14th century. The mosque's primary dome, fabricated from turquoise tiles, stood tall toward the blue sky, a true wonder of structure.

As they endured their journey, the tourists discovered approximately the effect of the Silk Road on Samarkand's way of life and financial device. The city's rich data and colorful culture were a testomony to the legacy of the Silk Road, and the vacationers felt privileged to have expert it firsthand.

Little did they recognize that their adventure had only without a doubt began, and there have been more wonders and mysteries to find out at the Silk Road.

The legacy of Genghis Khan maintains to encourage and impact humans nowadays, because it has for hundreds of years. From his incredible army strategies and conquests to his effect on Mongol way of life, the Silk Road, and modern-day times, Genghis Khan's effect can be seen in severa components of our lives. Despite the controversies and criticisms surrounding his management and strategies, his unwavering strength of mind and management have left a mark on records that can not be neglected. His tale is a reminder that one character, with courage, imaginative and prescient, and perseverance, can accumulate wonderful things and leave a long-lasting impact on the area. As we preserve to test his life and legacy, we are able to look at precious commands about management, way of life, and the strength of self-control.

Genghis Khan in Literature and Pop Culture

In a much-off land, there lived a first-rate ruler whose name became Genghis Khan. He changed into brave, robust, and effective, and his people cherished and feared him in same diploma. His name emerge as appeared in some unspecified time within the destiny of the arena, and reminiscences of his deeds have been suggested from era to era.

Genghis Khan have become a person of many talents. He modified proper right into a remarkable warrior, a wise ruler, and a professional diplomat. He knew how to win the hearts and minds of his humans, and he usually positioned their desires before his private. He modified right into a real chief, and his legacy would possibly endure for centuries to return back lower back.

As the years handed, Genghis Khan endured to boom his empire, conquering new lands and peoples with every passing day. His armies had been unstoppable, and his enemies trembled at the mere factor out of his call. But at the identical time as he grew extra powerful, he in no manner forgot the instructions he had located as a more youthful guy. He knew that actual greatness got here now not from the power of one's armies, but from the strength of one's character.

And so, at the same time as Genghis Khan died, his legacy lived on. His empire endured to thrive, and his humans endured to prosper. They remembered him as a incredible ruler, a realistic leader, and a real hero. And no matter the reality that he changed into prolonged long beyond, his name may usually be remembered as one of the fine in statistics.

Once upon a time, in a much-off land, there lived a exceptional ruler whose call turned into Genghis Khan. He grow to be brave, sturdy, and effective, and his humans cherished and feared him in same degree. His call grow to be stated at some stage in the arena, and recollections of his deeds have been suggested from era to generation.

Genghis Khan have become someone of many competencies. He have become a exquisite warrior, a wise ruler, and a professional diplomat. He knew a way to win the hearts and minds of his human beings, and he typically positioned their goals earlier than his very personal. He emerge as a real chief, and his legacy would undergo for masses of years yet to come again.

As the years passed, Genghis Khan persevered to extend his empire, conquering new lands and peoples with every passing day. His armies had been unstoppable, and his enemies trembled on the mere point out of his name. But even as he grew greater effective, he in no way forgot the schooling he had decided out as a young guy. He knew that real greatness came no longer from the electricity of one's armies, however from the power of 1's man or woman.

And so, while Genghis Khan died, his legacy lived on. His empire endured to thrive, and his human beings persisted to prosper. They remembered him as a super ruler, a clever leader, and a actual hero. And despite the fact that he emerge as long lengthy past, his name could likely continuously be remembered as one of the excellent in records.

As lots as the thriller surrounding the feasible life of a hidden treasure of Genghis Khan has captivated the overall public creativeness, students have remained skeptical. The loss of any concrete proof, mixed with the severa myths and legends which have grown around the determine of the outstanding conqueror, has made it hard to cut up reality from fiction.

However, some historians have recommended that Genghis Khan may moreover have indeed accrued a great fortune for the duration of his conquests, likely within the form of valuable metals, gemstones, and extraordinary valuable devices. While some of this wealth might also want to had been distributed among his loyal lovers, it's also feasible that part of it modified into set apart for the Khan's non-public use or hidden away for safekeeping.

One idea is that Genghis Khan might also additionally have created an difficult device of hiding places and mystery vaults, identified exquisite to a pick out few relied on people. These hiding places could have been positioned in faraway regions of the empire, or even past its borders, making it hard for simply every person to find out them.

While there is no concrete proof to help this concept, the truth that Genghis Khan modified into regarded for his cunning and strategic questioning shows that he can also furthermore have taken steps to guard his wealth and make sure its safekeeping for future generations.

Whether or not the treasure of Genghis Khan in fact exists, the iconic fascination with the possibility of its discovery speaks to the lasting legacy of the splendid conqueror and the iconic effect of his existence and achievements on the area.

Genghis Khan's dying and burial net website on-line stay shrouded in mystery and speculation. According to a few ancient payments, he died in August 1227 on the equal time as essential a military marketing campaign within the course of the Western Xia dynasty. The specific motive of his death is unknown, with some sources claiming he fell off his horse all through conflict and suffered lethal injuries, on the equal time as others endorse he may moreover moreover had been assassinated by his personal men or died of natural causes.

After his loss of lifestyles, his body have turn out to be another time to Mongolia, in which he have end up buried in an undisclosed region. The specific region of his burial net web site stays a topic of lots debate and hypothesis. Some believe he modified into buried in a mystery location within the Khentii Mountains, where a memorial turned into later built in his honor. Others declare he modified into buried in an unmarked grave in the Ordos Desert, or that his remains were scattered in accordance with Mongol manner of lifestyles.

Despite numerous efforts over the centuries to find Genghis Khan's burial net web page, it remains undiscovered to in the intervening time. In present day years, some researchers have used satellite television for laptop tv for pc imagery and particular advanced era to search for the tomb, but thus far their efforts were fruitless. The mystery surrounding his final resting place has satisfactory added to the legend of Genghis Khan, cementing his popularity as one in every of records's maximum enigmatic and fascinating figures.

Burial (Fiction)

As the solar started to set at the massive Mongolian steppe, a hard and rapid of mourners accumulated around the body of Genghis Khan. The Great Khan, who had conquered vast territories and united the nomadic tribes beneath his rule, grow to be useless.

But even in loss of life, Genghis Khan have become now not to be underestimated. As the mourners watched, the floor beneath his body started out out to tremble and shake, and a effective magical power started to emanate from the corpse.

Suddenly, a big stone tomb seemed out of nowhere, developing up from the ground to encase Genghis Khan's body. The tomb modified into protected in complicated carvings and symbols, and modified into covered via powerful magical wards that could hold the Great Khan's stays safe for eternity.

The mourners stood in awe as they watched the tomb disappear back into the earth, leaving no trace of its lifestyles inside the again of. And so Genghis Khan, the effective conqueror, emerge as buried in a way befitting his greatness, his legacy covered by way of manner of the handiest of magical enchantments.

Chapter 15: The Early Life Of Genghis Khan From Humble Beginnings To Rising Power

Genghis Khan is a call that is synonymous with strength, conquests, and the introduction of a awesome empire. However, before he have grow to be the ruler of the largest empire the sector had ever seen, Genghis Khan have become a younger boy from humble beginnings. This essay will discover the youngsters of Genghis Khan and the manner he rose to energy from his humble beginnings.

Genghis Khan have emerge as born in 1162 in the rugged terrain of Mongolia. He become born with the decision Temujin, which means that "iron employee," and turn out to be the second one son of his parents. His father, Yesugei, have become the leader of the Kiyad tribe, and his mother, Hoelun, have turn out to be from the Olkhonud tribe. However, Genghis Khan's formative years changed into some distance from easy. When he have become simply 9 years antique, his father emerge as poisoned with the resource of rival tribe individuals, and his circle of relatives modified into left with out a protector.

At a younger age, Genghis Khan determined to be impartial and innovative. He needed to rely on himself and his mother to survive inside the harsh Mongolian landscape. He observed the manner to hunt and fish, and he also determined out a manner to adventure horses, which have end up a crucial talent in his future conquests. Genghis Khan's youngsters changed into full of hardships, but the ones reports should form his character and make him a effective chief inside the future years.

As Genghis Khan grew older, he started to say himself as a pacesetter. He collected a small organization of enthusiasts, which blanketed his brothers and one of a type people of his tribe, and he began out to profits conflict in competition to neighboring tribes. He modified into decided to avenge his father's lack of existence and come to be the leader of his tribe. He modified into a hit in his efforts, and with the aid of the age of 20, he had end up the leader of the Kiyad tribe.

However, Genghis Khan's desires did not prevent there. He knew that he had to expand his territory and benefit greater energy if he grow to be going to live on inside the competitive global of Mongolian politics. He fashioned alliances with one-of-a-type tribes and began to revenue conflict in competition to large and similarly powerful tribes. His army processes were cutting-edge and effective, and he rapid received a reputation as a professional and ruthless warrior.

One of the key moments in Genghis Khan's rise to energy became his victory over the Tatars, a powerful tribe that had been raiding Mongolian settlements for years. Genghis Khan led his military to victory closer to the Tatars, and he obtained a huge quantity of booty and slaves. This victory cemented his recognition as a powerful and professional leader, and it furthermore gave him the belongings he needed to hold his conquests.

Genghis Khan's conquests persisted through the years, and he slowly but clearly expanded his empire. He conquered neighboring tribes, and he moreover started out to invade China. His conquests have been no longer pretty plenty gaining territory, however furthermore approximately spreading Mongolian lifestyle and traditions. He created a crook code, which come to be based on Mongolian customs and traditions, and he additionally recommended exchange and commerce inside his empire.

Chapter 16: The Formation Of The Mongol Empire Strategies And Tactics

The Mongol Empire grow to be one the numerous most vital empires in facts, spanning within the course of Asia and Europe. It became formed through a aggregate of military conquests and diplomatic alliances, and its success turn out to be in massive component due to the techniques and techniques employed thru its leaders. In this text, we will discover the formation of the Mongol Empire and the techniques and methods that have been used to create and hold it.

The Mongol Empire come to be founded by using the use of manner of Genghis Khan inside the early thirteenth century. Genghis Khan turned into a expert warrior and chief who turn out to be able to unite the nomadic tribes of Mongolia underneath his rule. He become a hold close of method and strategies, and he hired a number of present day strategies to build his empire.

One of the key strategies employed through Genghis Khan changed into his use of a enormously cell and flexible navy. The Mongol army have become made from cavalry, and they had been capable of flow into short and with out hassle at some point of the open steppes of Mongolia. This mobility modified into a key advantage, because it allowed the Mongols to attack their enemies from surprising angles and to keep away from getting bogged down in extended sieges.

Another key method employed through Genghis Khan modified into his use of psychological war. The Mongols have been recognized for their brutality, and they'd frequently have interaction in techniques which consist of using captured prisoners as human shields or impaling their enemies on stakes. These strategies were designed to strike fear into the hearts in their enemies and to lead them to greater willing to surrender.

In addition to his navy techniques, Genghis Khan changed into furthermore a professional diplomat. He become capable of shape alliances with neighboring tribes and global places, which helped to enlarge the Mongol Empire. He became furthermore recognized for his ability to delegate authority, which allowed him to interest on strategic alternatives and to go away the regular manipulate of his empire to his subordinates.

After Genghis Khan's demise, his empire became divided amongst his sons and grandsons. These successors continued to use the strategies and techniques which have been hired thru Genghis Khan, and that they have been able to hold and boom the empire. One of the critical element strategies utilized by Genghis Khan's successors changed into their use of siege battle. The Mongols have been able to use their superior engineering talents to collect siege engines and to breach the walls of fortified towns.

Another key tactic employed by using Genghis Khan's successors become their use of divide and conquer techniques. They may want to frequently play rival factions against each special, and they'd use spies and informants to accumulate intelligence on their enemies. This allowed the Mongols to strike at their enemies when they have been at their weakest and to gain a bonus in battles and campaigns.

The Mongol Empire eventually got here to an quit within the 14th century, however its legacy endured to be felt for centuries. The techniques and strategies hired via the Mongols might have an effect on navy questioning around the area, and they may encourage one-of-a-kind conquerors together with Tamerlane and the Ottoman Empire.

Chapter 17: Genghis Khan's Military Campaigns Conquests And Triumphs

Genghis Khan, the founder of the Mongol Empire, changed proper into a navy genius and a great strategist. He become capable of unite the nomadic tribes of Mongolia and assemble a huge empire that spanned across Asia and Europe. Genghis Khan's army campaigns were characterised by using way of pace, flexibility, and brutality. In this newsletter, we're capable of explore Genghis Khan's army conquests and triumphs, and the way he become capable of build one in every of the most vital empires in facts.

Genghis Khan's navy campaigns started out out in the early 1200s. His first conquests were closer to neighboring tribes in Mongolia. He speedy found out that a mobile cavalry army turned into his greatest asset, and he used this to his benefit in battles. The Mongol cavalry turn out to be capable of circulate short throughout the open steppes of Mongolia and release marvel attacks on their enemies. Genghis Khan modified into also a draw near of mental war. He may also want to often use brutal strategies, which embody impaling his enemies on stakes, to strike fear into their hearts and to lead them to extra inclined to surrender.

After consolidating his electricity in Mongolia, Genghis Khan grew to become his attention to neighboring worldwide locations. His first predominant campaign changed into towards the Khwarezmian Empire within the Middle East. The Khwarezmian Empire turn out to be taken into consideration one in every of the maximum important and wealthiest empires of the time, but it end up no in shape for the Mongol cavalry. Genghis Khan's military modified into able to flow into rapid at some point of the desolate tract and launch a surprise assault on the Khwarezmian capital. The town have become short taken, and the Khwarezmian Empire became destroyed.

Genghis Khan's subsequent conquests have been closer to China. The Chinese Empire have come to be one of the excellent empires in the global, but it changed into weakened via using internal strife and corruption. Genghis Khan's army became able to exploit the ones weaknesses and triumph over lots of northern China. The Mongol conquest of China modified into characterised by means of siege conflict, with the Mongol navy using superior engineering skills to construct siege engines and breach the walls of fortified cities.

Genghis Khan's navy campaigns were no longer restrained to Asia. He moreover sent expeditions into Europe. The most famous of these become the invasion of Russia. The Russian princes were capable of located up a robust resistance, however they have been in the long run defeated by the use of the Mongol navy. The Mongols continued their conquests into Europe, subsequently carrying out as some distance west as Hungary and Poland.

Genghis Khan's military campaigns were marked thru numerous triumphs. One of his best triumphs become the conquest of the Khwarezmian Empire. This conquest introduced substantial quantities of wealth and territory to the Mongol Empire, and it solidified Genghis Khan's function as one of the satisfactory conquerors in history. Another triumph have become the conquest of China. The Mongol conquest of China delivered an surrender to centuries of Chinese dominance and mounted the Mongol Empire as a primary international power.

Genghis Khan's military campaigns have been now not without their traumatic situations. The Mongol military faced many difficulties, which incorporates harsh terrain, immoderate weather conditions, and properly-prepared resistance from their enemies. However, Genghis Khan have grow to be capable to overcome those traumatic situations via his tactical brilliance and his capability to conform to converting situations.

Chapter 18: Genghis Khan As A Visionary Leader Political And Social Reforms

Genghis Khan end up not exceptional a tremendous navy strategist and conqueror however additionally a visionary leader who applied political and social reforms that had a profound effect at the Mongol Empire and beyond. His reforms helped to create a unified Mongol u . S ., sell spiritual tolerance, and set up a sincere and truely prison device. In this article, we're able to find out Genghis Khan's political and social reforms and their lasting legacy.

One of Genghis Khan's most large political reforms have turn out to be the appearance of a centralized authorities. Before his reign, the Mongol tribes were loosely prepared, and there has been no essential authority. Genghis Khan found out that a unified Mongol country required a strong tremendous authorities. He mounted a device of neighborhood administration, with governors and judges appointed to manipulate justice and collect taxes. He moreover created a tool of communique, with a community of roads and relay stations to facilitate the short transfer of information and orders.

Another important political reform come to be the advertising of meritocracy. Genghis Khan believed that management positions ought to be primarily based totally on benefit, in place of social fame or own family ties. He appointed human beings based totally on their competencies and skills, irrespective of their records. This helped to create a greater inexperienced and effective authorities, further to to sell social mobility.

Genghis Khan emerge as additionally a champion of spiritual tolerance. In a time even as religious variations regularly brought on warfare, Genghis Khan believed that people have to be free to worship as they pleased. He promoted religious freedom inside the path of the Mongol

Empire, and his tolerance prolonged to all religions, including Buddhism, Christianity, and Islam. This policy helped to foster a experience of concord and tolerance in the Mongol Empire, as people of numerous religions have been able to stay and work collectively in harmony.

Genghis Khan additionally applied large social reforms. One of his maximum crucial social reforms come to be the introduction of a sincere and in reality crook system. He set up a code of prison suggestions, referred to as the Yasa, which included the whole lot from property rights to criminal law. The Yasa modified into based totally totally mostly on the standards of justice, equity, and equality, and it helped to ensure that everybody, regardless of their recognition, were handled similarly underneath the law.

Another critical social reform become the advertising of schooling. Genghis Khan believed that training turn out to be critical to the success of the Mongol Empire. He installed a tool of training that modified into open to all, regardless of their social recognition. He additionally recommended the interpretation of spiritual and philosophical texts into Mongolian, which helped to promote literacy and intellectual development.

Genghis Khan's political and social reforms had an extended-lasting impact on the Mongol Empire and past. His promoting of spiritual tolerance and meritocracy helped to create a greater cohesive and unified society. His established order of a honest and simply crook machine helped to sell justice and equality. And his advertising of training helped to foster intellectual improvement and growth the Mongol Empire's cultural achievements.

Chapter 19: The Legacy Of Genghis Khan: Impact On History And Culture

The legacy of Genghis Khan is one that has had a profound effect on every records and way of life. As a conqueror, he created simply one of the maximum vital empires the arena has ever visible, and as a leader, he carried out political and social reforms that helped to shape the future of his humans and beyond. In this newsletter, we are able to find out the lasting legacy of Genghis Khan and his impact on facts and way of life.

One of the most extraordinary legacies of Genghis Khan turn out to be his creation of the Mongol Empire. At its pinnacle, the Mongol Empire protected a vast territory that protected contemporary-day-day China, Korea, Russia, Eastern Europe, and the Middle East. This empire modified into one of the most essential and maximum numerous in records, and it delivered collectively people of various religions, cultures, and ethnicities below one rule. The Mongol Empire set up a extraordinary buying and selling community that facilitated the change of merchandise, thoughts, and technology among brilliant regions, and it paved the manner for the development of the current worldwide.

Genghis Khan's army conquests moreover had a profound impact on facts. His army campaigns had been marked thru cutting-edge strategies, together with using cavalry, and his armies were a number of the most disciplined and well-prepared in facts. Genghis Khan's conquests had an extended-lasting impact at the regions he conquered, and they induced the political and social systems of these regions for hundreds of years to head back.

In addition to his military conquests, Genghis Khan additionally completed political and social reforms that helped to form the future of his people and beyond. He created a centralized government, promoted meritocracy, and installation a honest and simply prison device. He moreover promoted non secular tolerance, which helped to foster a enjoy of group spirit and tolerance within the Mongol Empire.

Genghis Khan's legacy is likewise contemplated inside the lifestyle of the regions he conquered. The Mongols added their very personal unique manner of lifestyles, language, and customs to the areas they conquered, and moreover they accompanied some of the customs and traditions of the peoples they conquered. The Mongol Empire had a profound impact at the art work, track, literature, and structure of the areas it conquered, and it helped to create a rich and severa cultural legacy that also resonates nowadays.

One of the maximum lasting legacies of Genghis Khan is the impact he had at the development of the modern international. The Mongol Empire done a crucial role in the development of global change, and it facilitated the alternate of products and thoughts amongst special areas. The Mongols moreover helped to spread technology and improvements, which consist of gunpowder, paper, and printing, which had a profound effect on the improvement of contemporary civilization.

In end, the legacy of Genghis Khan is one that has had a profound impact on each records and manner of lifestyles. His navy conquests created one a number of the maximum critical empires the arena has ever visible, and his political and social reforms helped to form the destiny of his humans and past. The Mongol Empire hooked up a wealthy and severa cultural legacy that also resonates in recent times, and it helped to pave the way for the improvement of the modern international. Genghis Khan's effect on statistics and subculture is sincerely excellent, and his legacy stays felt round the sector.

Chapter 20: The Myths And Legends Surrounding Genghis Khan: Separating Fact From Fiction

Genghis Khan, the founder and primary emperor of the Mongol Empire, is one of the most iconic figures in information. His navy conquests and political reforms helped to shape the course of information, and his legacy continues to encourage people spherical the world. However, over the centuries, many myths and legends have emerged round his existence, making it difficult to cut up fact from fiction. In this text, we will discover a number of the myths and legends surrounding Genghis Khan and study the quantity to which they're based on historical reality.

Myth: Genghis Khan end up born with a blood clot in his hand, which changed into seen as a signal of his destiny as a superb conqueror.

This myth is one of the most well-known related to Genghis Khan, and it's far frequently mentioned as proof of his divine proper to rule. However, there can be no proof to signify that Genghis Khan modified into born with a blood clot in his hand. In truth, there are few dependable assets on his youth at all, masses of what we apprehend approximately him comes from later money owed.

Myth: Genghis Khan become a ruthless and bloodthirsty conqueror who showed no mercy to his enemies.

While Genghis Khan come to be honestly a expert navy strategist and conqueror, the idea that he turn out to be a ruthless and bloodthirsty tyrant isn't always completely correct. He became identified to be a honest and just ruler, and he accomplished reforms that progressed the lives of his people. He changed into moreover tolerant of various religions and cultures, and he advocated alternate and change interior his empire.

Myth: Genghis Khan changed into an illiterate barbarian who relied absolutely on brute pressure to triumph over his enemies.

This fantasy is often perpetuated with the useful aid of folks who view the Mongols as uncivilized savages. However, Genghis Khan was in fact a fairly wise and strategic chief who accomplished a number of present day-day techniques in his military campaigns. He became moreover seemed for his diplomatic abilities and his potential to unite disparate agencies of human beings under his rule.

Myth: Genghis Khan modified right right into a womanizer who had hundreds of wives and concubines.

While it is right that Genghis Khan had more than one higher halves and concubines, the concept that he had masses of them might be an exaggeration. In fact, he is believed to have had only a few dozen better halves and concubines over the route of his existence. It is likewise nicely simply worth noting that during Mongol tradition, it become now not unusual for rich and effective men to have multiple higher halves and concubines.

Myth: Genghis Khan was liable for the deaths of heaps and masses of human beings.

While it is right that Genghis Khan's army conquests resulted within the deaths of many humans, the idea that he modified into without delay responsible for the deaths of hundreds of heaps is in all likelihood an exaggeration. It is hard to estimate the appropriate sort of casualties because of his campaigns, but maximum historians be given as actual with that the death toll grow to be in the hundreds of heaps instead of tens of millions.

Chapter 21: Genghis Khan's Personal Life: Family, Relationships, And Legacy

Genghis Khan is thought normally for his navy conquests and political reforms, but his private life come to be also an critical element of his legacy. In this text, we're able to find out his own family, relationships, and the legacy he left within the returned of.

Family

Genghis Khan become born in 1162 in what's now Mongolia. His father, Yesugei, have become a tribal leader, and his mother, Hoelun, became a member of the Merkit tribe. Genghis Khan had severa siblings, which include a more younger brother named Temüjin, who have to later emerge as one among his closest allies and advisors.

Genghis Khan had 4 better halves and loads of concubines over the path of his life, and he fathered numerous kids. His first partner, Börte, became abducted with the beneficial useful resource of a rival tribe and held captive for severa months earlier than being rescued thru way of Genghis Khan. She remained his number one partner at some stage in his life and bore him several kids, collectively along with his eldest son, Jochi.

Relationships

Despite his reputation as a conqueror and warrior, Genghis Khan became recounted to be a compassionate and empathetic leader. He have emerge as deeply dependable to his family and buddies, and he valued the opinions of these round him.

One of his most critical relationships end up collectively along with his mom, Hoelun. She changed into a effective affect on his lifestyles and encouraged him to be a sturdy and independent leader. He additionally had a close to dating along alongside along with his brother, Temüjin, who served as virtually one of his most relied on advisors.

Genghis Khan modified into moreover appeared for his diplomatic abilties, and he modified into capable of shape alliances and maintain relationships with specific leaders and tribes for the duration of his reign. He modified into mainly professional at using marriage alliances to cement political relationships, and he prepared marriages for severa of his daughters to effective leaders and allies.

Legacy

Genghis Khan's legacy extends an extended way past his military conquests and political reforms. He is respected in Mongolia as a country extensive hero and is credited with laying the foundation for the Mongol Empire. His impact on records stays felt these days, and he's remembered as one of the maximum important figures of the medieval period.

One of the maximum good sized elements of his legacy is the manner he transformed the lifestyle and society of the Mongol human beings. He implemented reforms that abolished traditional tribal hierarchies and installation a centralized device of presidency. He moreover advocated the adoption of a written language and a standardized tool of weights and measures.

Genghis Khan's legacy furthermore extends to his descendants. He fathered severa children, and a lot of his descendants went directly to turn out to be rulers and leaders of their very personal right. One of his most famous descendants is Kublai Khan, who dominated the Mongol Empire from 1260 to 1294 and is belief for his conquest of China.

Chapter 22: The End Of An Era: The Death Of Genghis Khan And The Aftermath

The dying of Genghis Khan in 1227 marked the prevent of an era in Mongol facts. His passing left a energy vacuum that is probably crammed thru his successors, however it furthermore ushered in a period of instability and uncertainty for the Mongol Empire.

Death of Genghis Khan

Genghis Khan died in August of 1227 at the same time as on a army marketing advertising marketing campaign in China. The precise purpose of his death is unknown, but it's miles believed to were the quit result of accidents sustained in struggle or an infection. His body have turn out to be decrease returned to Mongolia and buried in a mystery area, as changed into the custom for Mongol leaders.

Aftermath of Genghis Khan's Death

The demise of Genghis Khan left a leadership void that became to begin with stuffed by way of way of his eldest son, Jochi. However, Jochi had a contentious courting alongside along with his father and have become not widely regularly happening as his successor. Instead, the Mongol Empire become ultimately divided among Genghis Khan's 4 sons: Jochi, Chagatai, Ogodei, and Tolui.

This department of energy added about a length of instability and infighting a few of the Mongol leaders. Jochi's loss of life hastily after his father's best brought to the chaos. The closing 3 brothers battled for control of the empire, with Ogodei in the end growing because of the reality the victor.

Under Ogodei's management, the Mongol Empire accelerated similarly, conquering components of Europe, Asia, and the Middle East. However, this boom also led to extended cultural and religious tensions, due to the fact the Mongols encountered human beings of numerous faiths and beliefs. The Mongol Empire changed into recounted for its spiritual tolerance, however there had been notwithstanding the fact that instances of persecution and violence in opposition to spiritual minorities.

Legacy of Genghis Khan's Death

Despite the demanding situations and uncertainties that observed Genghis Khan's lack of lifestyles, his legacy persevered to shape Mongol lifestyle and society. He changed into reputable as a national hero and remains celebrated in Mongolia in recent times.

His descendants persisted to rule the Mongol Empire for numerous generations, together together together with his grandson Kublai Khan being likely the maximum famous. Kublai Khan is thought for his conquest of China and his reputation quo of the Yuan Dynasty, which ruled China from 1271 to 1368.

The Mongol Empire moreover left a lasting effect on global history. Its conquests and enlargement paved the manner for the spread of thoughts, technology, and cultures across Eurasia. The Mongols were recognized for their military prowess and organizational skills, and their techniques and strategies had been studied and emulated with the useful resource of various navy leaders for masses of years.

Chapter 23: Genghis Khan's Influence Today Lessons And Insights For Modern Leaders

Genghis Khan, the founder and number one emperor of the Mongol Empire, has had a protracted-lasting effect on world records. Despite dwelling more than 800 years within the beyond, his legacy and impact can nonetheless be felt in recent times. As cutting-edge leaders face new annoying situations and possibilities, there are treasured education and insights that can be gleaned from Genghis Khan's management style and achievements.

Leadership Style

Genghis Khan's control style was characterized with the aid of a sturdy consciousness on meritocracy and innovation. He valued talents and ability over social reputation or records, and he endorsed his fans to count on outside the sector and innovate new techniques and procedures for battle.

This advantage-based totally approach to management grow to be groundbreaking inside the context of the time, in which social recognition and birthright frequently decided one's opportunities and success. Genghis Khan's ability to understand and reward skills and capacity helped to gather a devoted and committed navy, which finished a essential position inside the expansion of the Mongol Empire.

Innovation

Genghis Khan became moreover a grasp of innovation. He became open to new thoughts and recommended his fanatics to anticipate creatively and strategically. He noticed the rate in adapting and evolving, and he grow to be continuously searching out new procedures to enhance and optimize his army and his strategies.

This emphasis on innovation is specially applicable for modern leaders, who face a hastily changing and unpredictable worldwide. In order to stay ahead of the curve, leaders need to be inclined to test with new strategies and mind, and they want to be open to comments and critique.

Tolerance

Another key problem of Genghis Khan's management fashion modified into his emphasis on religious tolerance. Although he changed into a devout Shamanist, he recognized the charge in allowing his topics to exercise their very non-public religions and ideals. This dedication to spiritual freedom end up revolutionary within the context of the time, in which spiritual persecution and intolerance have been commonplace.

Today, non secular and cultural variety are increasingly more crucial troubles for leaders to navigate. Genghis Khan's instance indicates that tolerance and attractiveness may be powerful machine for constructing a sturdy and numerous society.

Empowerment

Genghis Khan end up moreover a draw near of empowering his lovers. He diagnosed that management changed into not pretty loads giving orders, but approximately inspiring and permitting others to acquire their desires. He recommended his squaddies to take initiative and make alternatives for themselves, empowering them to act within the exquisite hobby of the army and the empire.

This emphasis on empowerment and trust is specially relevant for contemporary leaders, who need to navigate complex organizational structures and construct accept as true with with their companies. By empowering others and delegating responsibilities, leaders can assemble a lifestyle of responsibility and possession, that could cause more performance and achievement.

Legacy

Despite his arguable legacy and the atrocities committed with the beneficial resource of his military, Genghis Khan's have an effect on and legacy can nevertheless be felt in recent times. He turn out to be a visionary chief who transformed the arena in strategies which are notwithstanding the reality that being studied and debated. His classes and insights may be valuable for present day leaders who're searching for to navigate a complicated and unexpectedly converting international.

Chapter 24: The Controversies Surrounding Genghis Khan Criticisms And Defenses

Genghis Khan, the founder and number one emperor of the Mongol Empire, is a controversial figure in international statistics. While many understand his navy conquests and political accomplishments, others criticize his brutal techniques and the atrocities committed with the useful resource of his military. In this text, we will find out the controversies surrounding Genghis Khan, together with the criticisms and defenses of his legacy.

Criticism: Brutality and Atrocities

One of the maximum common criticisms of Genghis Khan is his brutal techniques and the atrocities devoted thru way of his military. His conquests frequently involved the slaughter of complete populations, and his armies have been notorious for their cruelty and violence. Critics argue that this violence modified into needless and disproportionate, and that it brought approximately untold struggling and devastation.

Defenses: Context and Historical Perspective

Defenders of Genghis Khan argue that his moves want to be understood inside the context of the time. Warfare inside the 12th and thirteenth centuries come to be often brutal and merciless, and lots of different conquerors and empires engaged in similar techniques. Furthermore, a few defenders argue that the brutality of Genghis Khan's conquests changed into essential with the intention to set up a stable and unified empire.

Criticism: Treatment of Women and Slaves

Another criticism of Genghis Khan is his remedy of women and slaves. His armies often engaged in rape and sexual slavery, and he himself is said to have had many higher halves and concubines. Critics argue that this behavior modified into morally reprehensible and perpetuated a way of life of misogyny and objectification.

Defenses: Cultural Norms and Progress

Defenders of Genghis Khan argue that his behavior should be understood within the context of the cultural norms of the time. In the twelfth and 13th centuries, girls and slaves have been regularly dealt with as assets or commodities, and sexual slavery became commonplace. Furthermore, some defenders argue that Genghis Khan's empire in fact represented a form of development in phrases of women's rights, as girls had been regularly given big energy and autonomy inside the empire.

Criticism: Religious Persecution

Another criticism of Genghis Khan is his religious persecution of positive businesses. While he come to be fairly tolerant of non secular diversity, he moreover focused and persecuted specific non secular agencies, particularly the Muslims of Central Asia. Critics argue that this persecution grow to be unjustified and fueled religious tensions and violence.

Defenses: Strategic Necessity and Political Realism

Defenders of Genghis Khan argue that his actions have been driven by way of strategic necessity and political realism. The Muslim states of Central Asia were seen as a ability chance to the stableness of the Mongol Empire, and Genghis Khan's movements had been alleged to neutralize this risk. Furthermore, a few defenders argue that the non secular persecution emerge as not as immoderate as a few bills advocate, and that Genghis Khan in reality endorsed non secular tolerance and diversity inner his empire.

www.ingramcontent.com/pod-product-compliance
Lightning Source LLC
Chambersburg PA
CBHW071441080526
44587CB00014B/1943